Vortices and Spirals

Chapter 1

Transcending Time

We have a dynamic and vital relationship with Mother Earth that goes far beyond the air we breathe, the water we drink and the food we eat. Mother Earth nourishes us with a host of energies and essences that few know about let alone understand. She even nurtures our soul.

We also have a special bond with Mother Earth whereby we can co-create with Her a new birth that benefits both Her and humankind. One such bond is one I hold very dear—what dowsers call an energy vortex. Energy vortices are powerfully transformative, healing, and have a unique way of transcending time by connecting us to people in the past. To better understand this I would like to share with you an experience I had one summer.

My years of meditating in the woods have made me sentient of Mother Earth and sensitive to the thought forms that cling to the land. Unfortunately much of the Earth is blanketed with negative thought forms that can give me a headache. When I left my home in upstate New York to speak at a conference in Vermont this particular summer, it did not take more than thirty minutes of driving on the New York State Thruway before my head began to hurt. Fortunately, when I arrived in Vermont I was able to find a campsite that was not cluttered with negative thoughts.

The vibe at the conference center of this large ski resort was bad. After spending all day there I did not feel well so I decided to go for a hike and meditate in the woods. My intuition told me there was a

1

particularly nice place nearby so I decided to use my dowsing rods to direct me. As I began climbing, my dowsing rods pointed to my right hand side—indicating my meditation location was in that direction. When I reached the ridge trail connecting several peaks, my rods pointed to the left, indicating I should take the trail. Then they immediately returned to pointing to the right. When I climbed a small peak my rods went totally perpendicular. I followed my rods and turned right and walked off the trail; now my rods were pointing straight ahead. I continued walking until they opened up (180°) at a small semi-clearing near the edge of a steep drop-off. This was the place I had been looking for.

I sensed there was something special about the place as it felt so good to be there. Indeed my dowsing rods indicated a positive energy vortex had formed in this spot as they spun around in a clockwise manner. This is called an energy vortex because energy spins around in a whirlpool-like pattern. Energy usually travels in straight lines, so vortices are something unique. I call them natural vortices because they form naturally in

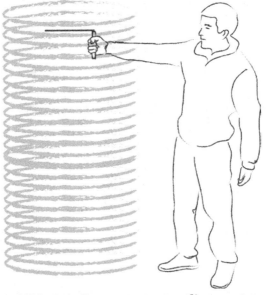

Exhibit 1-1. Geomancer standing next to an energy vortex clasping an L-rod (see Exhibit 1-2.) Notice the vortex is shaped like a column and not like a funnel

cooperation with Mother Earth from praying, meditating, selfless acts and positive intentions.

What may have once been a clearing with a spectacular view was now overgrown and blocked by several large trees. I surmised it was the once majestic view that attracted people to this mountaintop spot. Given the size of the trees, I estimated the vortex had formed at least a few hundreds years ago, and was created by the prayer and or ceremony of Native Americans. The vortex could have been much older and been reinvigorated by the continual praying of generations of Native Americans. There was no way of knowing for sure.

What mattered more than who created the vortex or its age, was it was very powerful. As soon as I began to meditate within it I could feel my subtle body being purged of the negative thought forms I had picked up the last few days. As I got deeper into trance I began to sense a variety of new and different sensations beyond my normal experiences during meditation. Seemingly, my soul was glowing and being nourished by the energy vortex. I was connecting with the vibe and essence of those who helped form this wonderful vortex. That is the beauty of a natural vortex; it transcends time and carries forward the consciousness, intentions and aspirations of all those who helped create it.

I stayed there for forty-five minutes and would have remained longer if evening was not about to descend. Before I left I gave heartfelt blessings and thanks to those who had worked with Mother Earth to create such a divine structure. My meditation buoyed me for my talk the next day as well as the trip home.

During my morning meditation at home on Monday I realized how much I had been blessed by my experience on the mountaintop. Instead of having to work through the mental debris I normally acquire after traveling, I went immediately deep into trance. Because my subtle body and consciousness had been stretched in different ways, I felt fuller and more complete.

Natural vortices are like mother's milk. Science tells us we build up immunity by being breast fed by our mother when we are young. Similarly, when we meditate in a natural vortex, we are fortified by the consciousness, thoughts and intentions of those who created it. Clearly my mountaintop meditation had nourished me with things I needed or lacked.

Some of my most powerful spiritual experiences have been within vortices at sacred spaces in the woods and in hidden and out-of-the way places. By meditating in one you will be gaining from the years of effort and experience of those who helped create it. In many ways, you will be transcending time when you fuse with consciousness of those who created the vortex.

The formation of a natural vortex is a wonderful and splendid thing. The formation is also a major accomplishment, bringing innumerable benefits. The increased flow of energy from a vortex can help improve your health, raise your consciousness and hasten your spiritual development--among other essential gifts. I will teach you how to find energy vortices.

I will also teach you how to create a natural vortex. They are a wonderful tool you can use for your own betterment, the betterment of humanity and to heal Mother Earth.

I have incorporated lessons on various dowsing techniques that will help you in your study of vortices. Knowing how to dowse, particularly using L-rods will greatly facilitate your study of vortices.

While learning to dowse may appear to be a formidable task, there are local chapters of the American Society of Dowsers (ASD) throughout the USA as well as other dowsing organizations in countries all over the world. These organizations offer their members free dowsing lessons or ones for a nominal fee on a regular basis. Many of them will have members familiar with geomancy. Within an hour or two you will be an old hand. I have listed contact information for the ASD as well as some other useful dowsing sites in the appendix of the book. Being able to find vortices is a highly rewarding skill as I just noted with my mountaintop visit in Vermont.

I have included a chapter on how vortices can be used to improve your spiritual practice, enhance healings and help heal Mother Earth. For example, energy healers will learn about a tool they can use to gauge their ability and monitor their progress to become better healers.

When discussing creating and using vortices, I have included some of the knowledge I have learned over the years of healing and enhancing Mother Earth by working with stones. Working with stones and stone formations is an

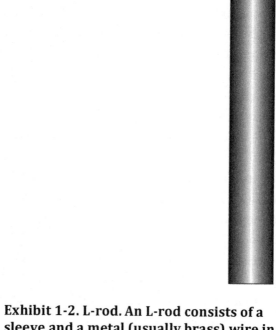

Exhibit 1-2. L-rod. An L-rod consists of a sleeve and a metal (usually brass) wire in the shape of an L that is generally several times the length of the sleeve. Most geomancers work with two L-Rods, one for each hand.

ancient art that facilitates a union with Mother Earth. Stone circles and megaliths are examples of working with stone.

While much of the focus of this book is on energy vortices, additionally on this journey you will get a better understanding of Mother Earth, a different take on consciousness and so much more.

Islam has a wonderful principle that each prophet must agree with the previous prophets, lest he be a false prophet. By agreeing with what has been said before, they corroborate and strengthen the teachings. The beauty of this book is it corroborates much of what so many faith traditions believe by showing you the mechanics of how those beliefs manifest in the unseen world. For example, throughout history prophets, sages and mystics have talked about the power of love. You will learn firsthand about the power of love to transform the world around you. Similarly, Hinduism and the New Age world speak about the concept of oneness, how we are linked to each other. I will explain to you several of the ways this oneness is accomplished.

Ultimately this is a book about our dynamic relationship with Mother Earth. Whether you are a dowser/geomancer, an environmentalist, a healer, a Gaia-based spiritualist, a dedicated spiritual aspirant, or an alchemist, your perspective regarding your discipline will be radically altered as you come to understand our dynamic relationship with Mother Earth. You will learn about the special bond we have with Her and the integral role she plays in our well being and spiritual development.

Before we can begin our study of vortices and spirals we first need to understand Mother Earth's unseen aspects. That is because a vortex exists in a higher reality.

Chapter 2

Consciousness Manifesting

Our daily life is filled with images of vortices from the mundane--the drain in our bathtub, to the spectacular—violent tornadoes and hurricanes covered by the media. What most of us don't realize is there are also a host of unseen vortices and spirals constantly swirling around us. We live in a world of invisible swirls, spirals and whirlwinds—some big, some small. It is these invisible vortices that are behind the ones whose force we can see. They all exert a tremendous influence upon us.

To understand these invisible vortices and spirals we need to examine the unseen world or what some have called 'Ultimate Reality.'

A Sea of Consciousness

We live in a sea of consciousness. Everything from our physical bodies, to animals, to mountains, at the core is consciousness, as well as our patterns of behavior and thinking. Sri Aurobindo, the great mystic and philosopher of the twentieth century, teaches "Consciousness is a fundamental thing, the fundamental thing in existence—it is the energy, the motion, the movement of consciousness that creates the universe and all that is in it – not only the macrocosm but the microcosm is nothing but consciousness arranging itself."[1] He believed the evolution of humankind hinges upon the transformation of our consciousness.

This sea of consciousness is all part of Brahman, or God, who is the source and end of all things. Brahman is the only thing that exists, the true reality, as the great Hindu sage, Adi Shankara, said, "All this universe known through speech and mind is nothing but Brahman; there is nothing besides Brahman."[2] Brahman is pure consciousness according to Shankara.[3] Because pure consciousness is Brahman it may be considered divine consciousness.

Reconciling the Unseen with Reality

Consciousness is pure spirit, yet we exist in a material world. How can this be?

Think of it like an interactive video game where everyone is represented by his or her own avatar. You control your avatar and others control theirs. In such a world there are two realities, one where the participants live, our physical world, and another imaginary world where the avatars interact with each other. Some may remember a similar situation in the movie, *The Matrix* (1999) where Neo, Trinity and Morpheus entered a simulated reality called the Matrix through interactive computers.

So it is with the sea of consciousness. Your true reality, or self, your soul, is pure consciousness and it exists in a spiritual world where everything is consciousness. At the same time you exist in a simulated reality—the material world. Your physical body is like the avatar in the video game.

The idea that the physical world is not real, is an illusion, is an old one. Hinduism calls it Maya. This is not to say that the physical world does not exist, but rather there is a greater reality behind it, consciousness.

Consciousness Defined

But what is consciousness besides spirit? We can begin to expand our definition of consciousness to say that it is awareness,

8

or where our awareness resides. Consciousness is what are we paying attention to, what are we experiencing, our focus. It is not so much that we may be aware of an object, but rather that we are focused on the object.

Go back to the interactive video where you control the avatars. When you are playing the game you are focused on the avatars and the simulated reality in which they exist. The more you concentrate and focus on the game, the more you become absorbed in it, and the more you become absorbed, the more you lose track of what is going on around you. Time can even begin to slip away as the world of avatars increasingly becomes your reality. Similarly it is with our true self, consciousness, and the material world. We are so swept up with the illusion of the physical world that we are unaware of our true self, consciousness. Instead our consciousness is focused on the material, and by embracing the material we make it our reality.

There are many more variations of consciousness. For our purposes we will define consciousness as where our awareness and what we focus on. Later I will further expand the definition of consciousness.

The Descent

If we exist in a sea of consciousness, and the physical world is like an interactive video game that is not real, how is the illusion of reality created? In order to achieve this consciousness must devolve and change its makeup to become more like matter and descend into the material pool. The Abrahamic tradition metaphorically speaks of our descent, with Adam and Eve falling from grace and being expelled from the Garden of Eden for having eaten the forbidden fruit.

Hindu Tantricism teaches that Shiva (consciousness) sends Shakti (energy) forth to create the material universe. The individual soul (jiva) is separated from the cosmic soul as it descends into the physical world.[4] Other Hindu schools[5] speak of how purusha (pure consciousness) and prakriti (energy) creates the material universe to help with its evolution and liberation.[6]

Consciousness, purusha and Shiva may be considered the same; similarly energy, prakriti and Shakti may be considered as being the same. Purusha is male, and prakriti is female; purusha is eternal, divine and prakriti is perishable and impermanent. Broadly speaking this means that consciousness makes up the spiritual realm (spirit) while energy primarily constitutes the physical world (matter.) This is a gross generalization but serves our purposes here.

To create the material world purusha must devolve and change its composition. This entails consciousness progressively diminishing its consciousness component and increasing its energy component. Prakriti becomes increasingly more pronounced the more it descends into the material world (Exhibit 2-1.) Less consciousness means the physical world is less spirit and consequently has less divine attributes. To better comprehend this think of energy as being matter.[7]

This is not to say the material world is nothing but pure energy; everything has varying degrees of consciousness. But rather, the world is gray and everything is made up of varying degrees of energy and consciousness, and the material world has a high energy, low consciousness makeup.

The descent into the creation of the material world is for the experience of the soul to illuminate itself. Prakriti (energy) exists for the pleasure of purusha (consciousness) who is the enjoyer[8], the divine witness. Because prakriti exists for the pleasure of purusha she is subordinate to purusha. In other words consciousness rules over energy, or energy serves consciousness and follows its will. This is an important concept, as you will later learn this principle is at work in an energy vortex. Consciousness rules and energy follows its will.

Prakriti is energy. She is also our material world; she is Nature; she is Bhu Mata (Mother Earth.) She is the Divine Mother, the creator of all. To pagans she is the Goddess. It is through the transformation of energy and other essences that she is able to create the material world.

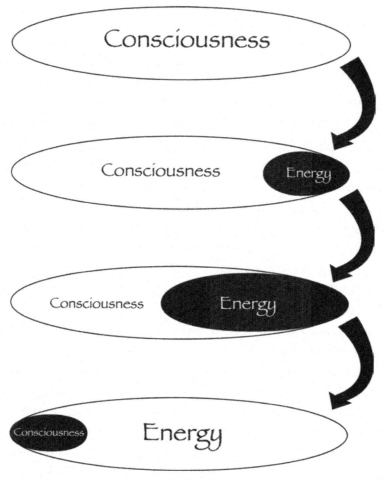

Exhibit 2-1 Consciousness Descending

The Great Division

As our consciousness descends into the material world we separate from God, Brahman, the cosmic soul. We also begin to fragment and develop the sense that we are independent, separate beings. The unity and oneness we had been experiencing is gone, yet there still exists a powerful unity, or oneness, amongst everything and everyone—we just don't realize it.

It takes an enormous amount of support apparatus to create the illusion of material reality. There are layers upon layers. These various layers may be lumped together by their function and can be called planes of existence (or just planes), or dimensions, or alternative realities. They are also planes of consciousness, each containing varying degrees of consciousness. There is a hierarchy within the planes of existence that can be viewed like a set of stairs with the plane closest to pure consciousness having the highest consciousness component and the lowest energy component. With each step down toward the physical world the consciousness component of a plane decreases and its energy component increases. The lowest plane is the Physical Plane and it has the highest energy and lowest consciousness component.

These planes of existence interpenetrate each other, interact with each other and influence each other. In other words we simultaneously exist in several realities that influence each other. Because higher planes have a higher consciousness component they rule over the lower planes; remember Shakti is subordinate to Shiva.

We will be primarily focused the Plane of Energy (Energy Plane) or Pranic Plane, immediately above the Physical Plane. Although the Energy Plane predominantly contains energy, the energy within it has varying degrees of consciousness. In Chapter 4, Our Bond with Mother Earth, you will learn more about the Energy Plane.

We have several bodies, or subtle bodies, what Hindus call koshas that exist in the various planes. Each plane has a corresponding subtle body. The physical body exists in the Physical Plane and the energy body exists in the Energy Plane. So while we are focused on the physical world and our physical body we have several other bodies that are simultaneously functioning in their respective planes of existence. The ones we will be most concerned with is our pranamaya kosha, or energy body that exists in the Energy Plane, or Pranic Plane and our physical body.

Vrittis

The various planes of existence and all their apparatus exist in the sea of consciousness we live in. Consciousness is still the ultimate reality, only now part of it has devolved into a variety of structures so our souls may be transformed through human experience. We still retain our higher reality of pure consciousness, but our awareness is focused on the material plane.

We create another layer of consciousness within the larger sea of consciousness through our thinking, actions and intentions. Our thoughts also bind together to create larger or collective thoughts. Some of these collective thoughts have been recognized and catalogued by science. There is what noted psychiatrist, Carl Jung, called archetypes that are reflective of the collective unconscious and shape our character and influence our behavior.

The sea of consciousness we exist in is dynamic and not static, but is constantly changing and evolving. Some, such as Jung, believed that the collective unconscious was static and set down from the earliest of time. I see our collective thoughts reflecting humankind's historical thinking and behavior and that it is continually being shaped by current generations. Everything is morphing, evolving or devolving; all are reflective of our collective psyche. Every being shapes and is shaped by our collective reality, both for the good and for the bad. This is a very dynamic process.

Hindus call our thoughts vrittis, literally translated as whirlpool. So consciousness in the form of our thoughts has a whirlpool, or circular-like pattern of movement. Vrittis[9] are vortices because of their whirlpool-like movement.

Given the form of consciousness is spiral-like or vortex-like, the sea of consciousness that we exist in is filled with swirls, spirals and vortices. We live in a world of vortices of which there is an almost infinite amount swirling around us.

The Spiral Form

Because consciousness has a circular or whirlpool-like movement, the spiral is the dominant form found in nature. We see it in water and in the air, with nature, with organs and more. Nature is replicating the underlying form of consciousness behind it. Obviously everything does not have a spiral form, but it is the dominant form found in nature. Author Geoff Ward echoes this in the title of his book *Spirals the Pattern of Existence*, and begins, "The spiral is the eternal, creative, unifying and organizing force or principle at work in the universe, and especially of ongoing creation of consciousness."[10]

Theodore Schwenk, a pioneer in the research of water and its form of movement, in his book, *Sensitive Chaos, The Creation of Flowing Forms in Water and Air* found that the inclination of water was to form and move in spheres and spirals. In endeavoring to form in spheres, water becomes "an image of the whole cosmos. If a directional force is added...then the combination of the two—sphere and directional force—will result in a screw-like or spiraling form."[11] This spiraling form is manifest in the movement of creatures in the water, and the formation of their organs through which water flows, such as gills. Because all living organisms pass through or remain in a liquid phase during their formation watery forms shape them.

Educator and mathematician, Michael S. Schneider, notes that the spiral is the most prevalent cosmic design:

> (They are) the purest expression of moving energy. Whenever energy is left to move on its own it resolves into spirals. The universe moves and transforms in spirals, never straight lines. Spirals show up as the paths of moving atoms and atmospheres, in molecules and minerals, in the forms of flowing water, and in the body of plants, animals, humans, and the greater bodies of outer space. A universal integrity of spirals unites all of creation.[12]

Energy is subordinate to consciousness (Shiva/purusha), so if energy is showing up in spiral forms, it is reflecting the consciousness behind it. Energy, like water, is reflecting and replicating the form of its underlying reality.

Replication

The idea that nature is replicating its underlying form, the spiral, is a key principle to understanding the material world. *The Emerald Tablet* says "As above, so below; so below, as above," credited to Hermes Trismegistus who is believed to have lived in ancient Egypt. He is considered the father of occult wisdom, the founder of astrology, discoverer of alchemy and the founder of the Hermetic Tradition.[13]

"As above, so below" implies that the microcosm is like the macrocosm. Similarly, the concept of replication states that the form and function operating at a higher plane manifests in a lower plane. Just as we breathe air in the Physical Plane, our energy body absorbs energy from the Energy Plane for sustenance. This is a very important concept that I shall be using throughout this book; that the form and function we see in the Physical Plane are similar to the ones operating in higher planes of existence as well. They are mimicking or imitating the form and function found in a higher plane of existence.

"As above, so below" says that there is a oneness and connection to everything and everyone.

Vrittis are the Building Blocks

Our thoughts, or vrittis, are the most elemental of vortices. They abound in an infinite amount around us. They also serve as the building blocks for more complex vortices such as energy vortices, samskaras and collective thought forms—each of which has a circular shape and a whirlpool or spiral-like pattern of movement like its parent.

Chapter 3

Vortices that Attach

Samskaras, Imprints & Talismans

Our thoughts, as well as the thoughts of others, can have a profound influence upon us. With an infinite amount of vrittis swirling about us, we are caught in a lot of whirlpools. This does not necessarily mean we are being influenced by all of them. There is only one type of thought we connect to because we are physically in its vortex; those are thoughts that attach to locations and objects where they were formed. We link up with other vrittis through our associations, focus and thinking, both conscious and unconscious.

Each time we have a thought, part of its being lingers and clings to where it was created. I call thoughts that attach to a particular location geographic samskaras; they may also be called land/geographic imprints, impressions, or memories. Through the reminder of this book I will refer to thoughts that attach to a location as geographic samskaras, or land imprints.

Thoughts that attach to objects are called talismans or amulets. Alchemists, wizards, and those practicing magic, have long understood that thoughts attach to objects, and created protective amulets and talismans to bring about good fortune throughout the ages. They did this through focused concentration upon the object that they wished to charge over an extended period of time. But it is not necessary to apply the focused intention of a sorcerer to create a talisman. We make them all the time.

This chapter will focus on thoughts that attach to places and objects.

Thoughts have Hurricane-like force

Thoughts are powerful and can exert a tremendous influence upon us. We need only think of their form to see this, a whirlpool. The image of a vortex has been used to describe incredible power through descriptions such as 'hurricane force' and inescapability with phrases such as 'death spiral' and 'spiraling out of control.'

Visualize a hurricane or a twister and you can see how powerful a force a thought can be. Anything within its whirlpool is in the grips of its force. If the object lacks strength or weight, it is at the mercy of the vortex and it can be tossed about like a peanut in a blender. While thoughts are not objects, as vrittis they do have a spiral form.

To understand vortices we need to know about thoughts. Thoughts have particular properties. Here are a few:

Prolific—Thoughts can reproduce faster than rabbits. They plant seed thoughts, or thought seeds, which look to influence our thinking or have us act upon them.

Growth Process—We give strength to a thought when we focus on it. The more we think about something, the stronger the underlying thought becomes, and the more it influences us, the more thought seeds it plants.

Control—Like weeds that can take over a garden, thoughts can take control of and dominate our mind, and have us thinking about them 24/7, blocking out other thoughts.

Law of Attraction—Like-minded thoughts are attracted to each other. We are drawn to people and places that are populated with similar types of thoughts. We bring into our life what we think about.

Morphing—Thoughts morph and can take on characteristics far different than when they were first formed. The Bhagavad-Gita says that "while contemplating the objects of the senses, a person develops attachment for them, and from such attachment lust develops, and from lust anger arises."[1] Anger can turn into violence, violence can turn into murder.

The Root of Karma

Hindu Vedanta teaches that each thought we have creates an impression on our mind called a samskara. These thought impressions, or samskaras, are like grooves on a vinyl album and are a permanent record of all that we think and do.

Not only does each thought we have create an impression on our mind, it also plants a seed, a thought seed that looks to multiply and produce more of its own by having us think or do the same thing over and over again. Who has not gotten a thought, or an earworm (song) in their mind that they could not shake? That is the power of a samskara. Its whirlpool pulls you into its web of thinking.

Each time we think or do the same thing repeatedly, the impression gets deeper and the samskara gets stronger. The deeper and stronger it becomes, the more powerful its influence is upon us. Samskaras limit our perspective and block out other thoughts. Meher Baba, the Iranian born Hindu mystic, who spent the last forty years of his life in a vow of silence, wrote that samskaras "form an enclosure around the possible field of consciousness."[2]

Because samskaras are a permanent record of our thoughts and actions, unless they are burned off or balanced through contra thinking or behavior before we die, we carry them with us into a future life. Samskaras are the root of our karma. Thoughts are truly powerful.

The Power of Place

Land imprints can have a profound influence upon us. Particular places we hold dear can sweep us up into their being and elicit powerful feelings and emotions. English Romantic poet William Wordsworth gives us a personal glimpse of the joy and wonderment he experienced in his youth communing with nature at Tintern Abbey[3] and how returning there brought it all back.

Five years have past; five summers, with the length
Of five long winters! and again I hear
These waters, rolling from their mountain-springs
With a sweet inland murmur.—Once again
Do I behold these steep and lofty cliffs,
Which on a wild secluded scene impress
Thoughts of more deep seclusion; and connect
The landscape with the quiet of the sky.
The day is come when I again repose
Here, under this dark sycamore, and view
These plots of cottage-ground, these orchard-tufts,...

He goes on to tell how the thought of Tintern Abbey gave him sustenance and the power to persevere during trying times.

If this
Be but a vain belief, yet, oh! how oft,
In darkness, and amid the many shapes
Of joyless day-light; when the fretful stir
Unprofitable, and the fever of the world,
Have hung upon the beatings of my heart,
How oft, in spirit, have I turned to thee
O sylvan Wye! Thou wanderer through the wood
How often has my spirit turned to thee!

20

I hope that you have a Tintern Abbey in your heart that you can draw upon. I have had many in my life and find they have changed, as I have grown older. Recently I drew solace from a sacred site that I hold very dear as I traversed through the dark night of my soul. It was during this time that the littlest emotion, the smallest fear, the tiniest guilt or anger would bubble up within me way beyond proportions. The flesh of my heart felt as if it had been rubbed raw or burnt by fire and was now being sanded by sandpaper. At those times I called upon God and remembered the joy and serenity I experienced so many times meditating on a stone by the side of a stream amongst old friends.

Each time I visit this place I am overwhelmed with joy and feel so blessed to be connected to it and be able to work to revive this holiest of holy places.

Conversely there are places that create dread within us, or can get us to think or do violent things. T. C. Lethbridge was a noted British archaeologist, and well-respected dowser, who bridged two worlds of the scientific and the occult. He applied his scientific approach to the investigation of the paranormal, and wrote several books in the mid-to-late 20th century on his findings. He believed a psychic field surrounds the human body and that we communicate to each other through these fields and through intermediary fields.

Lethbridge also believed the thoughts at a particular place could be very strong and get us to act in a certain manner. Once when he went to Ladram Bay in England to collect seaweed with his wife they experienced a queasy and depressing feeling near the face of a cliff. When they investigated the cliff above they felt as though someone put a thought into their minds to jump off. Lethbridge commented, "We were surely picking up the thoughts of someone who had either jumped off the cliff, or wanted to."[4] He noted that at least five other people had experienced a variety of similar occurrences and sights while there.

Land Imprints

Wherever we go, we are enveloped by the land imprints that are there. If we go to a divine place where people pray and meditate, then we will be uplifted; conversely, if we go to a place where violence has occurred, then we will be depleted.

The geographic samskaras at a particular place are a cumulative record of all that has gone on there. They are the sum total of all the actions and thoughts by all the individuals who have been there.

The particular thoughts that transpired at a location encourage us to do more of the same. For example, if you go to a place where someone has spent a lot of time thinking loving thoughts about a loved one, then that geographic samskara will try and get you to think loving thoughts of a loved one as well. The thoughts that make up a geographic samskara, are generic in nature, and are not a reflection of a particular loved one in this example, but the general idea of a loved one. Conversely, if you go to where someone has been attacked, the geographic samskaras there will try and force violent thoughts upon you. If someone who is already prone to violence goes there, then there is a chance he or she may not be restrained and will commit a violent act. That is why you often see repetitive violent behavior at the same place.

It is important to reiterate that there is a generic nature, or character to a land imprint that does not deal with specifics, such as a particular person or particular action. For example, as was just noted, if someone thinks loving thoughts for his or her partner, others that come in contact with the geographic samskara will think loving thoughts towards a loved one. When a geographic samskara influences a person to act, the action will be an unconscious interpretation of its underlying intent by that person.

Years ago I had made a welcome circle out of stones at the entry way to a sacred site. I spent a lot of time meditating and praying within the circle, focusing on introducing people to and preparing them for what was to come. The stones were buried in the ground and were barely noticeable. Years later I found that someone decided the entrance and welcome circle needed to be revived and resurrected it in a new fashion. The geographic samskara motivated them to build a set of small pillars.

Land imprints encourage repetitive behavior, increasing the chances that the same behavior will reoccur there. Research has found that the recovery of anesthetized mice improves if it takes place at the same location where other mice have recuperated.[5] Similarly, many spiritual teachers recommend we meditate in the same place to improve our meditative practice. In doing so we are making a thought form or geographic samskara at the space that encourages meditation.

The vibe or atmosphere you feel at a particular location is generally its land imprints.

Our environment can influence how successful we will be in changing a particular behavior, even incredibly addictive behaviors such as heroin addiction. A study by psychiatric researcher Lee Robins[6] for the Nixon Administration found that 20% of soldiers in Vietnam were addicted to heroin. Most stayed in Vietnam until they were cured. Surprisingly 95% of them remained heroin free after returning home to the USA. Compare this to a 90% relapse rate for those treated in the USA. The results were so startling that Robins spent years trying to defend that she was not lying or politically motivated.

Since then researchers have come to realize that our environment can influence the success of changing a behavior. Speaking to NPR Duke University psychologist David Neal said that, "[P]eople, when they perform a behavior a lot — especially in the same environment, same sort of physical setting — outsource the control of the behavior to the environment."[7]

While Carl Jung did not talk about geographic samskaras, he felt that land could have a profound influence upon us. When discussing foreign conquerors, he noted that ironically the consciousness of indigenous peoples covered the land and that "the foreign land assimilates its conqueror ....Our contact with the unconscious chains us to the earth and makes it hard for us to move."[8] In other words, the conqueror is conquered by the conquered whose thoughts and actions cover the land. While I think that Jung was referring to a larger collective consciousness, or unconsciousness of the land that went beyond a small samskara, it shows the power of our thoughts that attach to the land.

Talismans, Amulets

Our thoughts also attach to nearby objects. Everything—trees, cars, furniture and park benches, everywhere we go and everything we come in contact with will pick up our thoughts; as will objects that we carry like a purse or wallet and the clothes we wear. The greater the time we are in contact with these objects the greater our influence upon them.

Conversely the objects we come in contact with and carry exert an influence upon us. They are like the samskaras that attach to our subtle body and encourage repetitive behavior or thinking. How powerful an influence they have upon us depends upon the samskara attached to the object, how long we are in contact with it, its strength and our personal proclivity towards it.

The influence of our thoughts upon objects we come in contact with is profound, even our own body carries them. Organ recipients have reported what they call inherited memories, or cellular memories of the thoughts and memories of their organ donor. Claire Sylvia, a dancer, with a rare lung disease was one of the first recipient's of a heart lung transplant in New England in 1988 from an eighteen-year old man who had died in a motorcycle accident. In a post-operative interview with a reporter, she said she was "dying for a beer," something she did not like before her transplant. She also found herself drawn to other foods such as Snickers bars, Reese's Peanut Butter Cups, green peppers and Chicken McNuggets. These were foods she did not care for but were all favorites of her organ donor. She also found an increase in what she called male energy.[9]

In her book *A Change of Heart* she talks about other members in her support group who similarly found new influences and preferences thrust upon them after receiving their organ transplants. She even told how one of the group members went beyond preferences for new foods such as bananas and found character changes. Another person reported going to a church he had never been to before and feeling instinctively at home telling his wife he had been there before.[10]

Many occultists and mystics believe more than our thoughts attach to a particular object; that our whole life's trajectory, our past and future, attach to or can be accessed from our personal talismans.

Any object and even any material or substance retains and is influenced by our thoughts. Masaru Emoto, who captured the New Age world's imagination with his beautiful pictures of water crystals, believes that not only does water retain human thought but also its molecular structure can be shaped by it.[11]

We are creating talismans all the time. Later I will show you how you can create talismans, such as prayer stones, to clean space, protect and more.

Positive and Negative Samskaras

It is time to expand or qualify our definition of consciousness. Our thoughts have a morality to them, running along a continuum from the divine to the demonic (Bhagavad-Gita XVI.) We may broadly classify them as either love/selflessness (divine) or violent/selfish (demonic.) They may also be classified as positive or negative thoughts.

Positive thoughts adhere to the golden rule of "do unto others," act out of love and the interest of others; this is at the core of every faith tradition.[12] Negative thoughts are those that follow the law of self-interest, selfishness, and violence. All thoughts lie someplace along this continuum, with varying shades of being either divine or demonic, this consciousness permeates every piece of space on Mother Earth.

Positive and negative thoughts have different directional spins. Positive places and positive thoughts have a clockwise spin to them in the northern hemisphere and a counterclockwise spin in the southern hemisphere. Negative places and thoughts in the northern hemisphere have a counterclockwise spin and a clockwise spin in the southern hemisphere. An accomplished dowser will be able to gauge and discern the difference between positive and negative geographic samskaras. Their L-rods will mimic its consciousness, moving either clockwise or counterclockwise.

Why positive and negative thoughts have different directional spins in different hemisphere may have to do with the Coriolis Effect, or Coriolis Deflection. Science believes the direction of the spin of vortices is influenced by the rotation of the Earth and posits that inertia from the Earth's spin causes objects to deflect to the right. This influences vortices to have a counterclockwise motion in the northern hemisphere. Conversely objects in the southern hemisphere are deflected to the left. This results in a clockwise motion for vortices in the southern hemisphere. The Coriolis Effect is influenced by latitude; the closer an object is to the poles the more powerful the influence of the Earth's rotation.

The idea that our thoughts have a morality to them stands in sharp contrast to the theories of science that are focused exclusively on the material world. But observation of nature shows there are differences in the directional spin of vortices that can be classified as either positive or negative. The energy vortex in which I meditated in on a mountaintop in Vermont had a clockwise spin. Had I found a vortex in the southern hemisphere it would have had a counterclockwise spin. This vortex was formed from the positive intentions of prayer and ceremony and was incredibly uplifting and consciousness-raising. Similarly, just about every living creature with a spiral form has a clockwise shape to it. As Geoff Ward in his book on spirals notes, "[p]articularly at the microscopic level right handed or clockwise-turning seems to be favored by nature."[13] Conversely, tornadoes and hurricanes, which are incredibly destructive and violent, spin counterclockwise in the northern hemisphere.

Whether a particular place is, positive or negative is a cumulative record of all that has occurred there. That cumulative record contains both positive and negative thoughts that will influence your consciousness and thinking.

Centripetal versus Centrifugal

The difference between the physic's concepts of centripetal and centrifugal force sheds more light on the form and movement of positive and negative samskaras. Viktor Schauberger was a Bavarian born water magician, scientist, inventor and passionate nature lover. Through his intuition and time spent observing nature, and water in particular, he came to realize that centripetal movement was creative while centrifugal movement was destructive:

> The form of movement which creates, develops, purifies and grows is the hyperbolic spiral which externally is centripetal and internally moves to the center... [T]he destructive and dissolving form of movement is centrifugal in Nature—the forces moving medium from the center towards the periphery in straight lines.[14]

Basically Schauberger is telling us that the inward movement (centripetal,) what he called implosion, that mimicked the timeless wisdom of looking in[15] was the creative and positive force in nature. Conversely, the outward-looking movement (centrifugal,) what he called explosion, is the negative and destructive force in nature and focuses on the external world.

Schauberger believed that modern science and technology were built on the centrifugal movement of breaking down and destroying, through heat, combustion, explosion and expansion. The inefficiencies of modern technology had to do with nature's resistance to our destructive tendencies. He foresaw that our pursuit of technology would bring about ecological problems and strains upon humankind saying, "our technology points to death."[16] The result of which is cancer and other diseases, and the destruction of Mother Earth. Early on he concluded that we needed to have a symbiotic relationship with nature, otherwise we would bring about our own destruction.

A Geographic Samskaras' Form

A geographic samskara has the shape of a circular whirlpool (see Exhibit 3-1.) While it does not have a funnel-like eye, it does have a center, one that a geomancer can find. It gains strength through human intention or action that parrots, or mimics, its behavior or thinking. You can get a rough gauge of geographic samskara strength by measuring its diameter or radius.

The size of a geographic samskara can vary from being infinitesimal to miles or even larger in diameter. They tend to cluster together because they are self-reinforcing. There are also samskaras within samskaras, small pockets that go against the grain of the larger samskara that envelops them. Samskaras are localized consciousness, but can be very, very big.

28

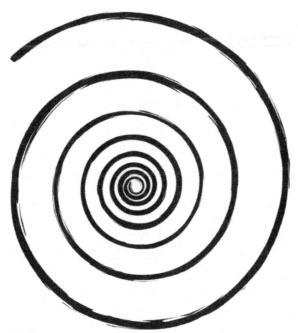

Exhibit 3-1. Geographic Samskrara. Top Down view.

The basic components of a samskara are:

Circle—The outside boundary of the samskara, the farthest reaches of its whirlpool, its size. It does not per se have a formal boundary, or a fence-like boundary.

Spiral, Vortex, Whirlpool—The swirl that makes up the samskara.

Eye, Center—The center.

Directional Spin--- The spin is either clockwise or counterclockwise.

Consciousness—Its morality, either positive (divine consciousness) with a clockwise spin in the northern hemisphere, or negative (demonic consciousness) with a counterclockwise spin; a general overall reading. It can further be broken down into positive and negative components.

Diameter, Radius—How wide the samskara is.

Geographic samskaras are dynamic and are constantly being shaped by what happens and what is thought at a particular place. We influence them and they influence us.

Formation and Conflict Resolution

Land imprints form everywhere but are the strongest where a particularly powerful emotional event has occurred, where the same behavior or thought has transpired over a long period of time, or where a strong contemplative mind has reflected on several occasions. Where you eat, sleep, meditate and go to the bathroom will have individual geographic samskaras. Some of them may cluster with other like-minded geographic samskaras in close proximity to each other. For example, if you meditate at different ends of a room, two geographic samskaras may form and over time they may unite to form a larger geographic samskara. This process can continue as other places where you or even your neighbor meditates are united to form an even larger geographic samskaras.

One of the features of land imprints is that they balance out and reflect a composite average of all that has transpired at a particular location. Theodor Schwenk, through his observation of flowing water, noticed that vortices formed within moving liquids as a way to resolve conflict and differences. For example, when flowing water enters a lake, vortices form at the periphery of the moving water. He called the formation of vortex to balance out differences the *Archetypal Phenomenon of Vortex Formation*;

> Wherever any qualitative differences in flowing medium come together, these isolated formations can occur. Such differences may be: slow and fast; solid and liquid; liquid and gaseous. We could extend the list; warm and cold; denser and more tenuous; heavy and light (for instance, salt water and fresh); viscous and fluid; alkaline and acid…At the surfaces of contact there is always a tendency for one layer to roll in upon the other. In

30

short, wherever the finest differentiations are present the water acts as a delicate 'sense organ', which as it were perceives the differentiations and then in a rhythmical process causes them to even out and merge.[17]

In other words the natural inclination of a flowing liquid when it is challenged and comes in contact with a fluid that is different is to attempt to balance out the differences. This is done by reverting to its underlying form, the consciousness behind it, a circle with a whirlpool-like movement. The whirlpool is the mechanism that brings about this merger of disparate elements. We can see a similar phenomenon with a blender or mixer that spins around various components to blend them together.

Calling it balancing may be too mild if we consider that water is mimicking its underlying form. A samskara looks to exert its control and influence; remember they are like weeds looking to overrun a garden.

The process of balancing that Schwenk describes is going on all the time around us. Wherever we go we all come in contact with geographic samskaras and talismans. The results are not necessarily a dramatic balancing or evening out, but there is an exchange of consciousness. This same merging and influencing goes on all the time with geographic samskaras.

Balancing out is a key feature of geographic samskaras and vrittis at large. This implies a dynamic process. Later you will learn how this balancing principle can be used to resuscitate and clear space.

The Unity Principle of Circles

Uniting disparate or different elements is a key feature of samskaras that is reinforced by their circular shape. The circle is a timeless symbol of oneness and unity. What Schwenk sees as the *natural inclination* of water to balance is a much more powerful force.

Consciousness seeks to unite and merge with all the other consciousness it comes in contact with, or anything within its circle.

This is a very important concept because it means we are constantly being shaped by the consciousness that we come in contact with, such as geographic samskaras and talismans as well as by the many circles in our life. By circle I mean the many relationships in your life. Each one of them at its core is a samskara with a powerful whirlpool and all its features. Just like any samskara their influence upon us will depend upon a variety of factors, such as its strength, our commitment to it, etc.

There are the larger collective thought forms such as archetypes that we connect to through our subconscious. There are also the many groups that we connect to (circles) because of our intentions, or actions such as whom we work for, our friends, the clubs we belong to, the products we buy, as well as our family and heritage. We also link up with distant talismans and places through our focus. There are almost an infinite amount of circles in our life. Think about something, see it, touch it and you are uniting.

When consciousness unites there is an exchange of the elements of each. We see the Unity Principle at work within a geographic samskara when it tries to influence our thinking and our consciousness quotient (see the next section that follows.) The inclination to unite, as seen in the flow of water, is evident throughout all of existence, as all of existence is consciousness. The Unity Principle is a strong force.

While a geographic samskara will try to merge with everything within its whirlpool, there are other independent geographic samskaras that remain within it. Tiny eddies and whirlpools resist by not blending with the larger thought form. In other words, some tiny individuality is retained within the larger collective; the self remains.

Influencing Our Consciousness Quotient

We are spiritual beings and our soul is pure consciousness. But part of our spiritual being is not pure consciousness and needs to be transformed—to become more loving, selfless, and giving—that is the purpose of our physical experience. Progress means expanding, or raising our consciousness.

To raise our consciousness our spiritual being has to become more like our soul, pure consciousness. Remember in the previous chapter I talked about how consciousness devolved to create the physical world by decreasing its consciousness component and increasing its energy component (Exhibit 2-1.) Similarly it is with our spiritual being, only in reverse. We must increase our consciousness component and decrease our energy component. We are not alone; everything needs to return home and become pure consciousness.

A rough reading of our progress is possible to get; in other words if 0 was pure energy and 100 pure consciousness, we could theoretically assign a number on a scale to measure our progress. I call it our consciousness quotient. It is a like temperature reading of your body, only it is measuring the consciousness component of your spiritual being and is a barometer of your progress or decline.

I am teaching you about your consciousness component not because I want you to be able to quantify it, but rather to educate you about how your environment and relationships, or circles, affect your spiritual development. They are constantly shaping you. The Unity Principle is at work 24/7, having your circles influence your thinking as well as influencing your consciousness quotient.

Whenever you travel you move through geographic samskaras, and come in contact with talismans that will either increase or decrease your consciousness quotient. Whether your consciousness is raised or lowered is a reflection of the relative difference between your consciousness quotient and the location's. How much your consciousness quotient is influenced will be a function of the samskaras strength, how much time you spend in it, as well as your affinity to it among other factors. For example, a brisk walk in cold weather will have less influence upon your physical body than standing still in cold weather for a long time. Each time you walk out the door, drive to work or the grocery store you are moving through a multitude of geographic samskaras--each one with a different reading, each one an influence. Unfortunately, most of the world is covered with negative geographic samskaras.

Similarly, the many circles in your life, from your family, friends, work and other associations will have a consciousness to them that will influence you. Understand, in many ways, you are a reflection of your circles.

You can get a rough reading of a geographic samskaras' consciousness quotient with a pair of dowsing rods, as I note in Exhibit 3-2 that follows. Positive places will spin clockwise and negative places will spin counterclockwise in the northern hemisphere. The speed of the spin will be a barometer of either the positive or negative features of a space. The faster that the rods spin the stronger the consciousness is.

Everything has a consciousness quotient or a consciousness reading because everything is consciousness and everything is evolving.

Apparitions

Samskaras can do more than influence our thinking and our consciousness quotient. Powerful geographic samskaras can make you see things. T C Lethbridge gave a variety of reasons for the sightings of ghosts and other apparitions. He believed that one of the reasons for someone seeing the classical vision of a nymph was because they were passing through someone else's thought field. As an example he told how an excited youth, resting within the static field of a stream, forms a very vivid mental picture of a girl bathing that leaks into the field of the stream and lingers there. A casual passer walks by the stream and picks up on the image in the field of the stream. The passerby believes he has just had a vision of a supernatural being when all he saw was a thought image.[18]

We Are One

We are one, part of Brahman, living in a sea of consciousness. Geographic samskaras are one of the ways we are linked to each other. Wherever we go, we are constantly coming in contact with the thoughts and consciousness of others. There is no escaping them.

They try to influence us by having us think or act in a certain manner. They also influence our consciousness quotient, for either the good or the bad. This has a significant bearing on everyone, particularly those of us who are dedicated to being more loving and making a better world and a better self. Similarly the many other circles in our lives influence us as well.

As much as we focus on raising our consciousness, we are constantly being shaped by the consciousness around us, which is generally not positive. Because of this, our consciousness quotient is being continually reduced as we go about our day. This raises a host of questions, such as; can we break away by ourselves, or do we need to focus on raising the consciousness of all on the Earth Plane for the collective good? I think the answer is clear—we are in this together!

Samskaras not only influence us but also have a dramatic effect upon Mother Earth, particularly on the movement of energy in the Pranic Plane. To better understand this I will next talk about our dynamic relationship with Mother Earth and how we affect each other.

Exhibit 3-2
Dowsing and Measuring
Geographic Samskaras

Learning to read land (or geographic) samskaras is a great way to connect with a place because it is a measure of its intrinsic character. However, this is not simple and you have to be an experienced dowser. I suggest you first try your hand seeing if you can find an Earth Chakra, see Exhibit 4-3.

I remember when I first learned about geographic samskaras at a sacred site that I hold dear. I was walking on a trail when all of a sudden my L-rods began furiously spinning around clockwise. I got all excited thinking that I had found a massive vortex. It was only after much reflection and study that I realized what I had been shown was the thoughts of those who had frequented this ancient sacred site.

This circular motion of geographic samskaras can be measured with a dowser's L-rods. To begin measuring the samskaras of a place ask spirit for help and guidance. With L-rods in hand I ask, "Please show me the samskaras." When you first begin I suggest you go someplace that should have a strong positive reading, a healer's table, a place of worship or where you meditate regularly. This should help you pick up on the vibe of the place. As you progress you will be able to measure samskaras every place you go.

Your first measure will be a net consciousness reading. In other words you will be recording the net difference between the good acts/thoughts and the bad acts/thoughts that have transpired at a particular location. If the good acts/thoughts far out number the negative acts/thoughts, you will get a strong positive (+, clockwise, counterclockwise in the southern hemisphere) movement of your L-rods. Conversely if the positive acts/thoughts are slightly less than the negative acts/thoughts that have occurred at a particular place, you will get a weak negative (-, counterclockwise) reading. This is a rough reading of the consciousness quotient of a place.

Your next measure would be to record the components (positive and negative) of your net samskaras reading. Ask spirit to show you the positive samskaras for a place. This will give you a reading of what good has transpired at a place. Next ask to be shown the negative samskaras.

Measuring the components of place is critical because many places can be conflicted. For example, you might get a weak positive reading. But when you ask to be shown the positive and negative components you may find there are both strongly positive and negative samskaras existing there. Such a reading would not be good because it would indicate there are strong negative influences lurking there.

The intensity of how positive or how negative the consciousness is at a particular place can be measured by the speed of a dowser's L-rods. The faster they move the stronger (positive or negative) the place is. This is a judgment measurement that needs to be calibrated by everyone individually. You need to develop this over time.

The land will begin to speak to you. Serene forests will show you their true beauty, while others will still register strong scars from de-forestation or the massacre of Native Americans, or you may find a hunter's tree stand in what is otherwise a positive setting. Sadly, much of what you will find will be negative. But when you do find a positive place as I did when I found a natural vortex on a mountaintop in Vermont the time and effort in learning to read land imprints will be well worth it.

Chapter 4

Our Bond with Mother Earth

She is our Mother; without Her, our existence would not be possible. All that we experience is a blessing from Her. Water, air and food are some of Her many gifts to us. She can nourish our soul and help transform us. She provides all of this so that we, humankind, can be transformed. The unseen world is Mother Earth.

She loves us. When we act like a foolish and arrogant child and oppose Her and harm Her, she still loves us. She still provides for us, nourishes and nurtures us. She is our Mother.

What we do and think matters to Her. Our thoughts and actions have a profound influence upon Her, which ultimately has a dramatic influence on us—for the good or for the bad. We are in this together; we are soul mates.

To learn how an energy vortex forms we need to understand our relationship with Mother Earth. In particular we need a basic understanding of the Plane of Energy.

She Makes the Illusion Possible

All of the planes of existence, all the layers upon layers and all the apparati is Mother Earth. If we return to the example of the interactive video game, Mother Earth is that video game.

When we play the interactive video game we are connected to it. We do this through the controls, which we operate and move about based upon our thinking and instincts. It is the same with our relationship with Mother Earth. She responds to our intention. Shakti is subordinate to Shiva and follows its will. We do this on the level of our conscious mind as well our unconscious mind. At the same time she responds to our collective mind, which controls much of our unconscious mind such as our form and movement.

So when we think something, whether it is consciously or unconsciously, Mother Earth responds. Our intention alters the simulation we call material reality the same way that the controls of our interactive video game affect our avatar.

A variety of reactions occur in response to our intention. One is that we attract energy, or prana, as you shall shortly learn.

The God Helmet

The idea that a burst of energy from Mother Earth can alter our perceptions of reality, or affect us in some other manner, can be difficult to fathom. However, there has been some scientific research substantiating that Earth energies can stimulate us and affect our thinking and senses. Cognitive neuroscience researcher, Dr. Michael Persinger,[1] has studied a myriad of unusual events— what may be called supernatural, paranormal or Fortean events; ghosts, UFO sightings, haunted houses and the like. While many have been fraudulent or been created by group think, or by the land imprints lingering at a location, he found many of these events were prompted by a burst of electromagnetic energy from Mother Earth. Not surprisingly, Persinger has training in geophysics.

In 1968 and 1969 thousands of people reported seeing the Virgin Mary and other angelic beings over a Coptic Orthodox Church in the Zeitoun district of Cairo, Egypt. Subsequently this Marian apparition has been named Our Lady of Zeitoun, El-Zeitoun or Zeitoun. Persinger examined seismological records and found there was a tenfold increase in seismic activity 400 kilometers southeast of Cairo. Critics of the electromagnetic theory for the sightings say that the tectonic shifts were too far away.

Persinger has created what is called a *God Helmet* a modified snowmobile helmet with attached solenoids located over the temporal lobes. It attempts to replicate the mystical experience by giving the wearer an increased jolt of electromagnetic energy. While many have reported the feeling of a sensed presence, or having an out of body experience, there are those whom have not.[2] Persinger dismisses the failures to an insensitive temporal lobe as well as other factors. Clearly Persinger is on to something.[3]

We are all the time getting jolts, bursts or just being in the flow of energy. Part of what I was experiencing during my mountaintop meditation in Vermont was an increased jolt of energy. That energy, however, had a much higher consciousness component than the energy Persinger works with.

To better understand the influence of Mother Earth's energies and essences upon us, as well as how vortices work, we need to examine the Energy Plane in detail.

The Plane of Energy

The Energy Plane, or the Pranic Plane is just above the Physical Plane and consists of energy. It is like a large body of water enveloping everything within it, physical objects, plants, flora and fauna with energy. At the same time, everything is made up of energy, or has an energy body. This energy is called the life force, prana in Hinduism and chi in Daoism. Without it we would die. It is said that the body will not die as long as it retains prana.[4]

The Energy Plane is the nuts and bolts behind the Physical Plane that makes material reality possible. Because it is so close to the material world in many ways, it is like, or is, the material world, only it is permeable and allows for pranas to interpenetrate each other. To comprehend how pranas interpenetrate each other, think of it like the air around us that allows various substances such as oxygen as well as other elements, water and manmade electromagnetic waves to coexist and not interfere with each other. One of the features of the Physical Plane is that the energy that comprises physical objects cannot interpenetrate each other.

There are a variety of structures in the Pranic Plane, performing a multitude of duties, from basic sustenance of our energy body, to helping with our spiritual evolution, to providing structure to the physical world among other things. All of these are dependent upon the movement of prana. When prana is not moving, it creates dead zones or worse. It is like electricity and needs to be moving in order to work. I believe that electricity is a prime example of the rule of replication. Electricity in the Physical Plane is replicating the movement and properties of prana in the Pranic Plane. Electricity is a power source that needs to be moving in order to power technology, otherwise we cannot turn on our electrical devices such lights or a computer. So think of the movement of electricity and its effect to understand prana and its movement.

At the most elemental level of the Energy Plane we are immersed in prana like a fish in water. When we are in a dead zone our energy body (pranamaya kosha) is not being properly fed the energy that we need to sustain ourselves. This ultimately filters down to our physical body because it is dependent upon the energy to power our physical body and give life to our organs. Richard Gerber, MD who wrote one the definitive books on energy medicine (*Vibrational Medicine*) advises that, "For good health to be enjoyed, one must have constant and unimpeded energy flow...If we are blocked in some way and thus impair the flow of energy at any level of the system, disease results."[5]

So the movement of prana is a critical component to our health and well-being.

There Are a Variety of Pranas

There are a multitude of pranas with a variety of purposes and functions in the Energy Plane. This goes against long-held beliefs that all prana are the same, they are not. There are a variety of prana. Each one is different and has its own unique purpose and function; some pranas nourish our energy body, others nourish our soul. It is important to reiterate again, there are variety of pranas; each is unique and having different qualities and functions.

One of the ways to distinguish between the different types of prana is to look at its consciousness component compared to its energy component. Is its makeup more energy or more consciousness? The higher the energy component, the closer the prana is to the Physical Plane, helping to sustain it and our energy body. The higher the consciousness component, the farther it is from the Physical Plane and the more that it serves higher purposes.

There is a wide variance in the consciousness component of pranas in the pranic plane. For example, Earth Prana has a very low consciousness component and is just about all energy. We are constantly immersed in it. I call it Earth Prana because it circulates in both the air and in the physical earth. This gives it sort of a dual purpose, above ground it nourishes the human energy body and the energy bodies of other members of the animal kingdom; below ground it nourishes the lowest forms of the material world.

Intention Driven

We are unconsciously constantly attracting a variety of pranas. Our intention and actions will dictate which type of prana we attract. Focus on the material world, and you will attract prana with a high energy component. Focus on the divine, and you will attract prana with a high consciousness component. Change your focus, and the type of prana you are attracting will change.

Earth Prana, as I mentioned, is coarse and contains a lot of energy. We are absorbing Earth Prana 24/7; it fuels our energy body and ultimately our physical body. We can increase the amount of Earth Prana that we attract through such things as when we get a healing from a hands-on healer, or energy healer. During a healing much of what a healer atracts is Earth Prana.

Conversely, when we meditate or pray we attract Cosmic Prana. Cosmic Prana has a high consciousness component and circulates strictly above ground. Cosmic Prana nourishes our consciousness quotient and our soul. It can help raise your consciousness.

Earlier one of my defining characteristics of consciousness was where our awareness was, or what our focus was. I defined it as such because what we concentrate on will determine what we attract and our view of reality. Our focus will attract a particular prana whose consciousness component will vary; it may also attract consciousness, various essences and may even block certain things.

Our intention is the KEY!

The Circulation Process

Prana is constantly moving. There are a variety of apparati and structures that facilitate the movement of prana. For example, ducts and chakras help move Earth Prana in the air around us. The process is very similar to a heating system of a home where ducts act like hot air registers that release Earth Prana and chakras (Earth Chakras) in the distance act like a cold air register that attracts the Earth Prana. This movement of Earth Prana across the surface of the Earth from ducts to Earth Chakras goes on 24/7 and fills every nook and cranny of the ether. There is another system that circulates prana in the land. This is one of the many systems in the Energy Plane that moves prana to nourish all of life and give structure and sustenance to the physical world.

A chakra is a vortex, or spinning wheel that draws prana towards it and in doing so helps with its movement. They are permanent structures in the Pranic Plane that cannot be altered the way that samskaras can. In other words they are static compared to samskaras that are dynamic.

Prana is drawn to a chakra by its clockwise spinning vortex. The whirlpool of the vortex draws in all the prana in 360° around the chakra. The chakra then funnels the energy into two energy lines at right angles to each other.

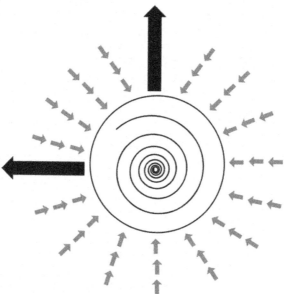

Exhibit 4-1. Earth Chakra: The diagram above is a top down view of an Earth Chakra. The vortex in the center (the circle) draws prana (broken lines) into the Earth Chakra and sends it into the Earth where it divides into two nadis, or energy lines (two thick lines) perpendicular (90°) that transport it a distance.

Prana Responds

The flow of energy does not take place in a vacuum, but exists in a sea of consciousness that has a profound influence upon it.

Geographic samskaras and talismans will affect the flow of prana; Shakti is subordinate to Shiva. Positive samskaras that are focused on the divine and service can enhance the flow of prana, while negative samskaras that are focused on violence and selfishness can disrupt the flow of prana. How much influence a samskara has on the flow of prana, as we shall learn in the next few chapters, will depend upon its strength.

Exhibit 4-2 shows how ever slightly a positive samskara can influence the flow of Earth Prana. It is a top-down view of a land imprint, or positive geographic samskara; the whirlpool which is spinning clockwise. The arrows are the Earth Prana that is moving from left to right, straight ahead.

Notice how the trajectory of the Earth Prana is disrupted near the center part the samskara; it is being pulled inwards toward the heart of the samskara. Energy is influenced by and follows thought.

The influence of our thoughts and actions upon the flow of prana can be much more dramatic than a slight pull or deflection. There can be places that have a great pull on the movement of prana as well as large dead spots where there are negative land imprints.

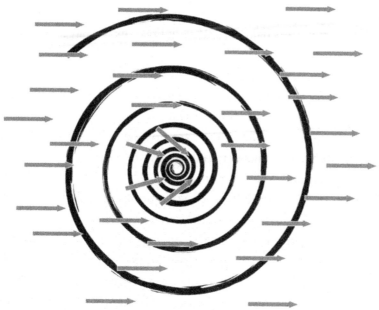

Exhibit 4-2. Samskara influencing the movement of prana.

Exhibit 4-3
Dowsing Earth Chakras

While finding an Earth Chakra requires some skill, there are variety of methods to accomplish your goal. Earth Chakras abound and you are probably within a few hundred yards of one right now. Learning to dowse for an Earth Chakra can help you in your ability to dowse for geographic samskaras.

Begin by asking Spirit to point your L-rods in the direction of an Earth Chakra and then follow them. Your rods will open up to 180° when you get to the Earth Chakra. Or upon finding an Earth Chakra your rods could also begin to spin, indicating a vortex, or open up at 90° degree angles to each other to dowse out the energy lines. Make sure you verify it is a chakra by dowsing out two energy lines at 90° to each other, otherwise you may have found some sort of other vortex, or chakra. Earth Chakras always have two energy lines at 90° to each other.

The chances are that many of you will not be able to find an Earth Chakra in such a fashion. However, you could begin by tracing out an energy line in the surface of the Earth. Most dowsers are able to find energy lines, they are not that difficult to find, or a more experienced geomancer could show you one.

Tracing out and following an energy line is a lot of work, but is well worth it. With some practice you should be able to find them on your own. This will involve some trial and error.

Once you find an energy line, begin by going in the opposite direction of the flow of the energy in the line. As you are following the energy line, look for other energy lines that are perpendicular offshoots to the energy line you are following. The perpendicular intersection should mark the end of one or both of them; it is actually the beginning. If you cannot determine the directional flow of energy within the energy line, you will have to do a trial and error of following the line one way and then the other way.

Chakras also come in a series that are all linked by the same energy line (See Exhibit 4-4.) Each of the individual charkas will have the main energy line below it, and an offshoot that is perpendicular at a 90° angle to the main energy line. So as you trace out your energy line look for offshoots that are perpendicular— they will come in a series of at least two or three offshoots equally spaced.

Once you find two perpendicular energy lines that you believe are part of an Earth Chakra, see if you can find a vortex above it. Your rods will be moving clockwise. Spend some time dowsing for a chakra as you might not pick up on it immediately.

If you are sentient of Mother Earth, or are a healer, you may feel the energy, which can affect you in several ways—a pickup in your energy, nervousness, and or a sharp sensation in your ajna charka (in the center of your forehead.) Another marker would be your dog getting hyper, as animals often get excited and energetic in an area with several Earth Chakras. My old dog, Kirby, would always get wound up and run around whenever we got into an area with several Earth Chakras. One spot on a particular trail always got him excited.

Once you find the Earth Chakra try and see if you can dowse the Earth Prana coming into it. Energy flows in 360° into the center of a chakra's vortex. Step three to five feet away from the center and the spinning vortex with one of your shoulders facing the center. Ask to be shown which way the Earth Prana is flowing. If your dowsing rods point towards the center you have been successful. You will probably not be able to do this the first time. But work on it and over time you will develop this valuable skill that will give you the ability to dowse the directional flow of Earth Prana wherever you are.

Spend some time on the chakra and keep dowsing in a variety of ways to develop your ability to find one without having to trace out an energy line.

To learn more about Earth Chakras see my youtube video: http://www.youtube.com/watch?v=XFNzglbm16o

.

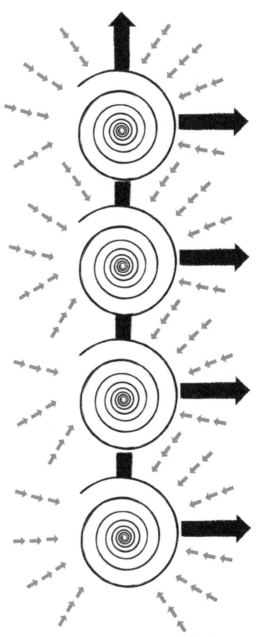

Exhibit 4-4. Series of Earth Chakras.

Chapter 5

The Birth of an Energy Vortex

A Co-creation with Mother Earth

As a positive geographic samskara gets stronger its influence on the flow of prana increases. For a positive geographic samskras this means that the amount prana drawn towards its center progressively grows. If it continues to get stronger it may eventually reach a critical mass and blossom into a vortex.

A vortex is formed when the consciousness of a geographic samskara creates a whirlpool of prana within a section of itself; in other words the movement of prana is spinning around and is mimicking the underlying movement of the samskara that is behind it. This increases the amount of prana drawn in at that particular location. This is how a positive vortex, or what I call a natural vortex, or what dowsers call an energy vortex, forms. The formation of a natural vortex, or energy vortex, takes time and effort. In Chapter 7, Negative Vortices, I will discuss the formation process of negative vortices.

The formation of a natural vortex is joint venture with Mother Earth. She has responded to our good intentions, our love, our compassion for all sentient beings and blessed us with a vortex. Starhawk, who is credited with revitalizing the pagan movement and the launch of the neo-pagan movement in the 1980's, says "the Goddess is immanent, but she needs human help to realize her fullest potential."[1] The birth of a vortex is also a celebration of the reunion of energy with consciousness, of purusha with prakriti, of Shiva with Shakti and is the beginning of many more co-creations and celebrations to follow.

The Formation Process

Positive geographic samskaras not only influence our thinking and our consciousness quotient, they also influence the flow of prana. As I noted in the previous chapter, we are constantly drawing energy to us, as well as a host of essences and consciousness, to us through our intention and focus. If our intention is positive, selfless and/or focused on the divine, Mother Earth may increase the flow of prana to us and eventually bless us with a vortex.

Each time we think or do something, we draw prana to us. Over time, repetitive thinking/action at the same location will create a strong mental imprint on the space that will linger there after we leave. In other words, remnants of our thinking and what it created or influenced will remain even though we are not there. For the movement of prana, this means prana that radiated towards us will continue to do so, only in a much more subdued fashion. Instead of a large pull of prana there will be a slight pull of prana in the immediate area of where we were, or in the center of the land imprint.

If we continue to feed the positive geographic samskara it will grow stronger and stronger and in doing so it will progressively increase the draw of prana towards its center. It takes time for a positive geographic samskara to increase in strength, and it will most likely remain at this pre-vortex level for a considerable amount of time and may never advance.

The first stage in the formation of an energy vortex begins with the creation of a vortex ring, a circling pattern of prana moving around the center of the geographic samskara independent of anyone being there. The prana is moving around like the clouds circling in the immediate area outside the funnel of a tornado, only it is spinning in a clockwise direction (counterclockwise in the southern hemisphere.) The ring is a fraction of the size of the geographic samskara.

A vortex ring will actually have prana moving around in a circular fashion, compared to the periphery of a geographic samskara that does not have formal ring, but only the farthest reaches of its spinning whirlpool/spiral. There will also be the nascent whirlpool-like movement of prana within the center. This whirlpool-like movement will become more distinguishable as the land imprint gets stronger.

The formation of a vortex ring arguably marks the birth of a separate but subordinate samskara. The vortex ring is a new samskara that is influencing the energy within it to move around in a whirlpool-like pattern. This samskara is not so much focused on the underlying intention as it is on the consequences of that samskara on the flow of prana in the Pranic Plane. By having the flow of prana move in a circular motion, the samskara is reverting to the natural shape of a thought form, a circle.

A vortex is formed when the geographic samskara begins to pull in all the prana within the vortex ring into its center, or eye. Again the vortex is a fraction of the size of the thought form, or geographic samskara and part of the geographic samskara. The prana is following the lead of the thought form, or the samskara. It is important to reiterate that the formation of a vortex is a result of the land imprint, the thought form to which it is responding. Energy follows thought.

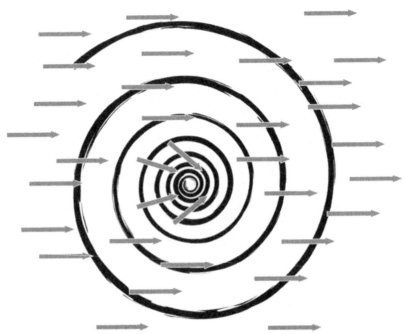

Exhibit 5-1a. Formation of a positive energy vortex begins when an imprint begins to influence the movement of prana. In the illustration above we can see the prana (arrows) moving straight ahead from left to right. In the center part of the imprint (whirlpool) some of prana (arrows) have begun tilting towards the center. The formation process begins in the center and expands out.

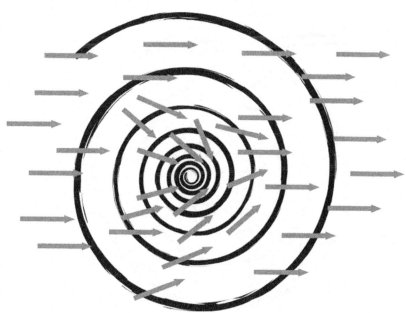

Exhibit 5-1b. The land imprint gets stronger. As the imprint gets stronger it will have a greater and greater influence upon the movement of prana. This means that the area of prana influenced by the imprint will increase, as well as an increase in the tilt of the prana towards the center ,the closer it is to the center. In other words, prana in the center area will have a greater tilt, draw or pull, towards the center, while the prana at the periphery will have a minimal pull or draw (tilt) towards the center.

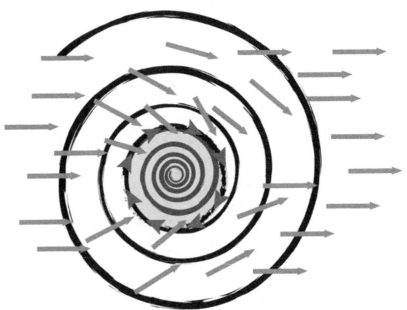

Exhibit 5-1c. The Formation of a Vortex Ring. The next stage in the birth of an energy vortex is the formation of a Vortex Ring; the circling of prana around the center of the land imprint. In the drawing above, the Vortex Ring consists of the arrowheads spinning in clockwise direction. Notice that just about all of the prana in the land imprint is influenced by it and the tilt of the prana has increased the closer that it is to the center.

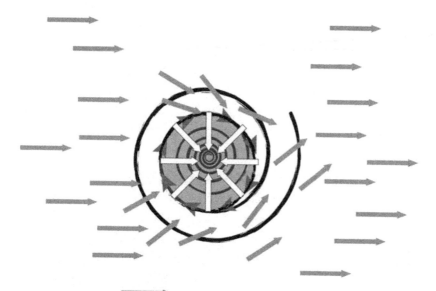

Exhibit 5-1d. A vortex forms. A vortex forms when all of the prana within the Vortex Ring radiates directly into the center of the land imprint. Basically the tilt of the prana closest to the center of the land imprint moves directly towards its center. All of the prana within the imprint is influenced by it (is tilted) and the degree of influence (tilt) has increased for the prana closest to the Vortex Ring.

57

In nature a vortex has a funnel-like shape with downward suction. Earth Chakras pull in prana and funnel it into energy lines, or nadis, in the surface of the earth. However, natural vortices of Cosmic Prana and Earth Prana appear to have a tall spinning column, rather than a funnel-like shape. One assumes that prana is pulled into the center of the natural vortex at a horizontal level.

Once Created

A vortex starts out small, a few inches or maybe a foot in diameter, at most. Over time it can grow much larger. I have dowsed vortices that are more than ten feet in radius. Because a vortex is part of a larger geographic samskara, it like all thought forms, or samskaras, gets bigger through repetitive behavior or thinking. The more that we feed the samskara the larger the vortex becomes.

Vortices can remain in existence for a very long time, hundreds of years if not longer. I have found vortices that I believe are thousands of years old at sacred sites. To me this demonstrates that they do not need to be nourished with thoughts and actions to remain active and alive as long as they are in a nurturing environment of like-minded consciousness.

However, negative (contra) thinking or behavior to the underlying geographic samskara will diminish the strength of a positive geographic samskara and natural vortex. It will take some time for the pull of a vortex to dissipate. It appears that the hurdle of creation, going from circling prana (vortex ring) to becoming a vortex, acts as a preventive for dissolution. In other words once created it is much more difficult to dissolve.

The disintegration process of a natural vortex is the reverse of the creation process. First the vortex dissolves, but the circular motion of prana and the vortex ring remains. Next the circular motion dissipates but there is a strong pull of prana. Finally there is no pull of prana.

Mother Earth Responds

Other formations may be simultaneously developing underground. Sig Lonegren, geomancer and author of *Spiritual Dowsing* has found that water domes and other features underground are drawn to sacred structures such as labyrinths and stone structures.[2] A water dome is a vertically rising stream that fragments into smaller fissures or streams as it rises; also called blind springs. Author Guy Underwood says that all prehistoric monuments were enclosed by blind springs, or spirals of water.[3] In her book, *Divining Earth Spirit*, Australian geomancer and author Alanna Moore wonders whether the monuments Underwood refers to were constructed on blind springs or blind springs were attracted to the monuments.[4] Her book mentions a host of phenomenon attracted to sacred places from spiral energy to nature spirits.

The birth of a vortex is celebration that brings the gift of an increased flow of prana from Mother Earth. There are many more celebrations with even greater gifts that can follow. One of which is the thinning of the veil, or reducing the barriers to higher planes of existence. I call this a Chimayo-Fatima, after two sacred sites, and is a common occurrence at holy places. A thin veil makes it easier to experience other realities and increases communication. Such gifts occur at the macrocosmic level with Mother Earth and they can accelerate our spiritual development.

The Anatomy of a Natural Vortex

The composition of an energy vortex is like that of a geographic samskara. It is circular in shape, has a spinning spiral or whirlpool, a defined width and a center, or eye. There are also some unique features to an energy vortex:

Vortex Rings—At the periphery of a vortex there is a ring of prana that circles clockwise around the vortex. It is the outside boundary of the energy vortex. The formation of a vortex ring precedes the formation of a vortex, indicating that formation of a vortex may soon follow.

Implosion, Radiating In—When a vortex is formed, prana begins to radiate in from the vortex ring 360° in straight lines within the space of the vortex ring.

There are also other swirls of prana within the vortex; rings or spirals that appear to be spiraling into the center, as if they are about to be pulled into the center. Jay Krappraff, writing about the spiral in nature, notes that all movement within vortices of water is not uniform and "is really divided into extensive inner surfaces, each rotating at various speeds. In the formation of vortices, these surfaces are drawn into the whirlpool."[5] It is the disparities in the speed of vortex rings in nature that give the vortex its corkscrew like appearances on the surface.

Speed—In nature, a vortex moves faster closer to its center. They obey Kepler's Third Law that planets move faster when they are closer to the sun.[6]

Energy Movement—Prana radiates toward the center of the vortex through a variety of paths:

Spiraling in—Prana follows a spiraling path into the center of the vortex.

Radiating in; from 360° within the vortex prana is flowing in a straight line towards the center of the vortex.

Mother Earth has other apparatus that recycles the prana pulled into an energy vortex. So the increased dose of prana moves into the vortex and then onward to someplace else.

Exhibit 5-2. Diagram of the movement of prana within an energy vortex. Prana circulates in variety of ways within a natural vortex.

Vortex Ring: The vortex ring is the outside periphery of an energy vortex where prana circulates in a clockwise manner as shown by the large arrowheads.

Whirlpools: There are a multitude of spirals within the area of the vortex ring spiraling clockwise into the eye of a natural vortex. The above diagram shows one them.

Radiating in: Prana radiates in straight lines into the eye of the energy vortex, as shown by the white arrows.

Talismans

Just as imprints attach to objects so do vortices form on objects as well. For example, energy healing is a strong and focused activity that creates a powerful imprint if done at the same place on a consistent basis. Imprints will form on both the practitioner's table and at the space where the healing occurs. Over time they may blossom into vortices.

The location of the vortex on an energy healer's table is generally around the heart, or head area. It will form where the healer places their hands most of the time during a session; if there are several areas of focus it may form in the center area of those healing areas. The practitioner's table should be viewed as a talisman. Energy healers should try and take their tables with them when they do healings outside of their office to take advantage of its properties.

Other alternative healers, such as chiropractors, will also have vortices form where they do healings. It takes a longer time for a vortex to form for other alternative therapies. This is because energy healers are intentionally working with the life force to pull it into their patient, while other alternative therapists are less focused on it.

An energy healer's table, or a place of healing, is one of the best places to try to feel or dowse for a vortex of Earth Prana (See Exhibit 5-3.) Make sure to try one that has been used for some time by an accomplished healer. It may well be that you or a friend has practiced some healings and that a vortex or a circling pattern has formed at the healing area. A circling pattern with a dowser's L-rods would indicate that there are vortex rings and a vortex may soon be born.

It helps to be a healer. To develop your sense of Earth Prana you may wish to begin by performing some healings yourself to try to feel the flow of energy into you. Such practice can be invaluable in developing your ability to feel prana. Once you can feel Earth

Prana, you can build upon that sensation to sense other aspects of Mother Earth.

A Beautiful Birth

The birth of a vortex is a beautiful and wonderful event that brings innumerable benefits such as an increased dose of prana as I will describe in the next chapter. In the chapters that follow I will give you advice on how to create vortices and talismans.

Exhibit 5-3
Sensing or Dowsing a Vortex of Earth Prana

Being able to sense an energy vortex begins by going to a location that has one. The most likely location will be the healing table of an accomplished Reiki or Therapeutic Touch practitioner who has been performing healings on the table for some time.

Start by asking the divine for help, then spend some time sitting or meditating on the table. If a vortex has formed it will most likely be in the head or heart area. That is where you should sit.

Now walk a little away from the table and then come back. When you come back lean over the area where you were sitting and simultaneously move your hands over the area as if you were in the dark fumbling for something. Focus on the sensations coming to you. Concentrate on those sensations. Generally a vortex of Earth Prana will energize you; it may give you tingling feelings. It could also be felt in your ajna chakra, or in the area slightly above the center of your eyes in your forehead.

Walk away again and then come back and see if you feel a difference. Keep going in and out of the vortex to see if you can feel a difference. Focus on the sensations that you experience, as this will strengthen them.

To dowse a vortex, ask to be shown the vortex. Your dowsing rods should point to an area of the healer's table. Walk to that area. When your rods open up, you are in the vortex. My L-rods generally open up at the area of the vortex ring. See if you can get one of your rods to show the spin of the vortex. They should spin clockwise. Try to find its center. See if you can find the outside edge of the vortex, or its vortex ring. Trace it out.

If you can do all that, try and see if you can get your rods to dowse the flow of Earth Prana into the center of the vortex. With your L-rods in the vortex ask to be shown the flow of Earth Prana. Your rods should point towards the center of the circle. Walk around the center and see if your rods keep pointing towards the center. This will help give you a sense of the flow of prana and help develop your feel for it.

If you are having difficulty dowsing out a vortex try finding one when a healing is going on. The increased energy flow will help.

I will teach you how to dowse for a natural vortex of Cosmic Prana in Exhibit 6-5 Sensing or dowsing a vortex of Cosmic Prana.

Chapter 6

Bathed in Bliss and Well-Being

The formation of a natural vortex is a wonderment of nature and a blessing from Mother Earth. It is quite an achievement and marks a new birth. An energy vortex can nourish us with an increased flow of energy that brings many benefits.

Your Circle with Mother Earth

When you are in a natural vortex you are in a positive geographic samskara so strong it has begun to manipulate the flow of prana within it. Clearly such a samskara is much stronger than one that has not formed a vortex and it will have a much greater sway upon your thinking and consciousness quotient. You need to realize that when you are in a vortex you are in a powerful samskara. The corollary to this is that a vortex is one barometer of the strength of a geographic samskara.

When you are in a natural vortex you are experiencing an increased flow of prana. This does not necessarily mean you are absorbing it. Like the bioavailability of vitamins and minerals, you have to be able to assimilate Mother Earth's essences to benefit from them. Your Gaia Connection/Circle, or your circle with Mother Earth, will determine how much of that increased prana flow you will absorb. It is based upon your sentience of Mother Earth, how sensitive you are to her and how strong a samskara you have developed to draw in her essences, energies and consciousness. Your sensitivity to that particular prana as well as you intention will also influence how much you will absorb. If you have a weak Gaia Circle and have not developed the ability to absorb a particular prana and are not engaged in activity that regularly attracts that particular type of prana, you will not absorb much, if any.

The more that someone is focused on a particular prana, the greater the chances are that they will absorb some. Intention will also increase the absorption rate for those who can absorb a particular prana. When I lead group meditations to teach people to connect with Mother Earth, I always ask them to focus on the sensations they are experiencing coming into their bodies as they are meditating. In do so they are giving strength to the nascent feelings that they are developing of Mother Earth. Learning to connect to Mother Earth is about developing a samskara to connect with her. Think of it like building a muscle or skill set. The more that you merge with Mother Earth's Circle the more that you will be able to absorb.

The conclusion is that in order to benefit from the increased energy flow of a natural vortex, you have to have some sensitivity to it.

An Increased Jolt of Prana

One of the basic premises of energy healing is to increase the amount of life force, prana, coming into the energy body. Therapeutic Touch developed by clairvoyant Theosophist Dora Kunz, and Dr. Dolores Kreiger, believes that illness is a result of the flow of energy being obstructed, disordered or depleted. To achieve well-being, practitioners employ techniques to remove obstructions and return balance as well as directing the life force into the patient. Being able to draw prana from Mother Earth is critical to a healer practicing Therapeutic Touch. Janet Macrae, a nurse and Therapeutic Touch practitioner, tells that a healer must be able to continually draw upon the life force in the universal field during a healing, otherwise he or she would quickly be depleted.[1]

Research of hands on healers finds there is a resonant link between patients and healers during the healing process. Both patient and healer show a 7.8Hz (cycles per second) brain-wave activity, which is the alpha theta interface and the Schumann Resonance of the Earth's magnetic field.[2]

Energy healers, whether they are practitioners of Reiki, Therapeutic Touch or BodyTalk, all draw energy to them when they do a healing. It is this increased pull of energy that contributes to the healing. Since their intent is to heal the physical body, they draw pranas that nourish the physical body, one of which is Earth Prana. As I noted earlier it circulates in both the air and in the ground and is a coarser and lower consciousness component prana.

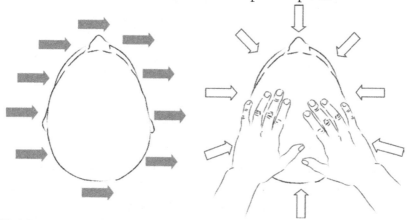

Exhibit 6-1. Healing draws Earth Prana. We are constantly in flow of earth prana (arrows) and absorb it 24/7, as seen in the drawing on the left side. During a healing the amount of earth attracted to us increases as shown in the drawing on the right with the healers' hands on the head.

Gauging a Healer's Draw, Ability

We are constantly attracting prana and consciousness 24/7. It radiates in from all directions 360° into us. Theoretically you could draw a circle around the periphery of a particular prana radiating towards someone. Our intention will determine the mix of what we attract. When we concentrate and are focused on one activity, we will increase our draw (how much we attract) of a particular prana. For example, energy healers will increase their draw of Earth Prana when they do a healing. This will increase the hypothetical circle that we could trace out of the prana radiating towards the healing. The larger the radius, or pull of Earth Prana during a healing, the more they are attracting. The radius of an energy healers' draw is one barometer that can be used to gauge their ability.

I have found wide variances in the ability of energy healers to draw Earth Prana. Some have had a draw of a little over one foot while others have had draws several times that. When gauging a hands on healer other factors should be considered. Healing is also about removing blockages, it also about an exchange of consciousness.

Vortex Synergy

When you perform a particular activity such as an energy healing, or meditating, within a vortex your draw of prana can double or more. This is because there is a synergy that occurs when your draw combines with the draw of the vortex.

An energy healer doing a healing within a vortex on a healer's table will have their draw of Earth Prana extend far beyond its normal distance. For example, if the radius of your draw is three feet you are pulling in prana from three feet around you. When a healing is done within a vortex of Earth Prana your draw of Earth Prana may increase to four, five, six or more feet in radius. The size and power of the vortex will greatly influence how much your draw increases. An increased draw will help with the healing.

Performing healings within a vortex can greatly enhance your healing ability. Other activities such as meditation can similarly be greatly enhanced when done within a vortex that draws in the prana that comes with meditation.

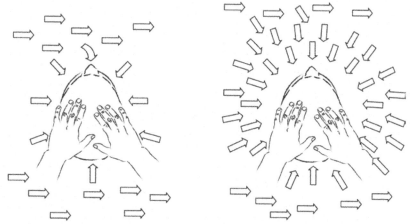

Exhibit 6-2 Vortex Synergy. The illustration above shows two healings. The one on the right is being done in an energy vortex of Earth Prana, while the one on the left is not. Both are attracting Earth Prana (arrows) but the one on the right is attracting much more, as it has a larger area of draw. Notice that both areas of prana drawn towards the healings have a circular shape.

Cosmic Prana

When we meditate or pray, our intention is focused beyond the physical world. We may be looking to help others, to communicate with God, or to improve our spiritual self. There are many other reasons for praying or meditating, but at a minimum our focus is transcending our physical being. Since our focus is not on physical reality, we do not attract Earth Prana.

Spiritual exercises such as meditation and prayer attract a prana with a much higher consciousness component, what I call Cosmic Prana. A vortex of Cosmic Prana takes quite some time and spiritual acumen to create. Consequently it is more enduring and resilient than vortices of other pranas that have a higher energy and lower consciousness component.

Neuroscientist Andrew Newberg and Mark Robert Waldman wrote a book about God and the affects spiritual practices have upon the brain. In *How God Changes Your Brain* they noted that "spiritual practices…enhance the neural functioning of the brain that improves physical and emotional health… Contemplative practices strengthen a specific neurological circuit that generates peacefulness, social awareness and compassion for others."[3] In other words, spiritual exercises raise our consciousness.

Underlying these changes to our brain is the increased flow of Cosmic Prana into our subtle body. When we meditate, we increase our draw of Cosmic Prana as Mother Earth showers us with more of it. Just as healing draws Earth Prana that feeds our energy body, spiritual practices increase our inflow of Cosmic Prana that feed our soul.

When we meditate or perform other spiritual activities within a vortex of Cosmic Prana or similar high consciousness component pranas, a synergy occurs with the vortex that greatly increases the draw of Cosmic Prana, or other high consciousness component pranas.

Pranas Interpenetrate Each Other

One of the rules of the planes of existence is that they interpenetrate each other, with the exception of the Physical Plane. Similarly, the various components of the planes of existence, such as various pranas, interpenetrate each other.

70

While a natural vortex of a particular type of prana will draw that same type of prana, it will usually not impact the flow of other pranas. For example, a natural vortex of Earth Prana will not affect the flow of Cosmic Prana and a natural vortex of Cosmic Prana will not affect the flow of Earth Prana.

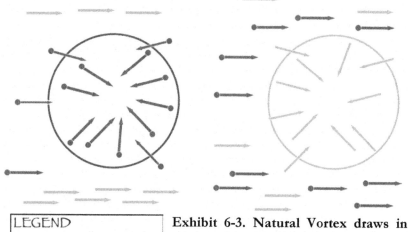

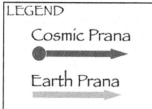

Exhibit 6-3. Natural Vortex draws in its intended prana. The above illustration is of two energy vortices. One is a natural vortex of Cosmic Prana (left) the other is one of Earth Prana (right.) Notice that the Comic Prana vortex draws in Cosmic Prana and has no influence on the flow of Earth Prana. Similarly the vortex of Earth Prana draws in Earth Prana and has no influence of the movement of Cosmic Prana.

A Spiritual High

Meditation can have a very positive influence on our feeling of well-being. How well it makes us feel can range from feeling good, to being blissed out and having a *spiritual high*. I believe a great deal of that feeling of well-being comes from the essences, energies and consciousness that Mother Earth showers us when we are focused on her, the divine or selflessness.

My years of meditating in nature have taught me that Mother Earth can profoundly affect how we feel. I have had moments meditating within her divine spots, and within vortices that have made me feel extraordinarily compassionate and loving towards even the most violent and cruelest of people. I have also experienced some of what I can only describe as a *spiritual high* when I felt incredibly ecstatic and would at times have visions. I was achieving these states because Mother Earth was showering me with her gifts.

While a vortex does not necessarily bring about such ecstatic states for everyone all the time, an increased dose of Cosmic Prana can surely improve you sense of well-being.

It is important to realize that we are supposed to feel good.

Improve Your Spiritual Practice

A vortex of Cosmic Prana whether at a sacred site or on a talisman, can significantly improve your meditative ability. The vortex brings the samskara of meditation and an increased dose of feel-good Mother Earth. It can also bring a part of those who helped create it.

Meditation is about building a samskara to be able to focus and tune out the outside world. One of the reasons we are told to meditate at the same place is to develop a geographic samskara at that location to help us advance in meditation. When you meditate you strengthen the thought form, or samskara of meditation, making it stronger. It is no different than any other thought form that grows from attention and thoughts focused on it.

Meditating within a vortex of Cosmic Prana, created from prayer or meditation, means you are meditating in the thought form of someone who has the ability to go deep enough into trance to create a vortex. When you meditate within such a vortex you are merging with a powerful samskara focused on meditation. Think of the Unity Principle. You will not be achieving the same states of consciousness or ability of those who created the vortex, but you will see your meditation improve as you are tapping into their samskara.

When you meditate within a vortex of Cosmic Prana created by someone else, you will also raise your consciousness. As I noted with my mountaintop meditation in Vermont in Chapter 1, I was benefitting from the effort and intention of those who created the vortex. This gave me a healthy dose of their consciousness. I was tapping into their circle and uniting with it and it was bathing me with them. This fusion gave me what I called a healthy dose of mother's milk. There is a mystical power that unity brings about.

Burn off Other Samskaras

The increased energy inflow from a vortex of Cosmic Prana can also help to burn off one's samskaras. As the great sage Shankara said; "As gold is purified through heating on fire gives up its impurities and attains to its own luster, so the mind, through meditation, gives up its impurities of Sattva, Tajas and Tamas, and attains to the reality of Brahman."[4]

When you perform spiritual practices in a vortex of Cosmic Prana, or other high consciousness pranas, you increase the amount of consciousness coming into you. This increased flow of high consciousness prana helps burn out your impurities.

The road to Samadhi and Enlightenment is about traveling through the dark night of our soul and the purging of our mental and emotional baggage. Meditating in a vortex of Cosmic Prana can significantly speed up your spiritual transformation.

We Are What We Absorb

Just as the health of our physical body is a function of what we eat and drink, so it is with our many other subtle bodies, or koshas, only they are a reflection of what we absorb. In fact, our higher bodies influence our physical body so what they absorb matters even more.

Before we can absorb something, we need to attract it, and we do this though our intention. If we focus on the material world, focus on money and wealth, or do violent or selfish things, we will draw high energy and low consciousness component energies,[5] or we may have certain pranas blocked. Conversely, if we focus on the divine, do good works, act selflessly and meditate, we will attract low energy and high consciousness component energies. The former will feed our energy body the latter will nourish our soul.

It is the absorption of high consciousness component energies such as Cosmic Prana that will increase your consciousness quotient and in doing so help with your spiritual evolution. Meditating in a vortex of Cosmic Prana can increase your intake of Cosmic Prana. More in this case is better. I can tell you first hand that having meditated in a variety of vortices and divine aspects of Mother Earth has greatly hastened my spiritual development as well as firmly connecting me to Mother Earth. Undoubtedly other variables, such as the many circles in your life, will influence your consciousness quotient, but increasing your dosage of high consciousness energies by meditating in a vortex of Cosmic Prana will be of significant help to you.

The corollary of this is that when we follow the teachings of the great sages and prophets and love, give, act selflessly or meditate we nourish our souls. In doing this we spiritually advance.

Feed Your Soul

Energy work is great. Learning to feel Earth Prana is wonderful. Pranayama is helpful and can be very therapeutic. Your energy body needs to be nourished. However, the focus of so many today on energy, its all about the energy, is worrisome. Our energy body undoubtedly needs to be fed but after a certain point all this energy work provides little if any benefit and can wind us up by giving us too much energy. You can become hyper. Instead you need to feed your soul.

Learning to feel and work with energy is a wonderful step in our spiritual transformation, but it is only one step. Pranayama is the fourth rung of eight rungs on Patanjali's system of yoga. It is only half way up; the four that follow are all focused on meditation.

Being able to sense and work with energy is a vital tool, but at some point you need to move on. You will also find that as you build your bond with Mother Earth, the benefits of energy work will diminish as you will get what you need 24/7 effortlessly.

Feed your soul.

Celebration

The birth of a vortex is a celebration that marks the union of purusha with prakriti, Shiva with Shakti, consciousness with energy.

Patanjali teaches the reunion of consciousness with energy is critical; "The purpose of union of purusha and prakriti is to experience the essential nature, and to achieve, in themselves, the powers or purusha and prakriti."[6] In his commentary of that particular sutra Swami Satyananda Saraswati the guru, yoga teacher and sannyasin notes that the undeveloped person has not unfolded the powers in himself or herself while the spiritual person has.[7] He implies the difference between the two is great because the powers are enormous. As the union of purusha and prakriti evolves, certain spiritual and supernatural powers come about and manifest in us.

Clearly the reunion of purusha/Shiva/consciousness and prakriti/Shakti/energy is critical to our personal spiritual evolution. Both Tantra and Patanjali speak to our individual spiritual evolution through reunion. But what about the larger world? If the macrocosm is like the microcosm then the reunion of two through our connection to Mother Earth must similarly occur in order to awaken us and unlock all sorts of spiritual and supernatural powers.

Next we I will talk about debilitating negative energy vortices. It is said that we need darkness in order to see the light. No doubt the benefits of natural vortices will become more apparent as we examine the horrors of negative energy vortices.

Exhibit 6-4
Measuring your draw of Earth Prana, or Cosmic Prana

Measuring an energy healers' draw of Earth Prana is one tool to objectively quantify his or her ability. It is also a valuable tool to measure your progress if you are a healer.

It is important to keep in mind that the location where you take your measurements can have a significant impact on your results. Test yourself at a neutral site. I recommend taking the average of at least three different locations. For example, if you are measuring in an area where healings have occurred, then your results will be skewed showing a greater radius. Conversely if you measure in an area that is troubled, and the flow of prana is disturbed, your results will be skewed to showing a smaller radius.

In order to measure an energy healer's draw you need to have the ability to dowse out the flow of Earth Prana with your L-rods. To get this ability I suggest you start with learning to work with Earth Chakras (Exhibit 4-3, Dowsing Earth Chakras); and develop the ability to sense and feel a vortex of Earth Prana, as well as the ability to dowse one before you begin. There are a variety of methods suggested by which you can do this. I recommend trying all of them.

Stand next to the healer. Start by trying to determine the directional flow of the Earth Prana where you are. Ask the Divine to show you which direction the Earth Prana is flowing. It will be flowing towards the closest Earth chakra—north, south, east, and west. This is not easy and you need to be an accomplished dowser. Let your rods point in the direction the Earth Prana is flowing.

Ask the healer to begin the healing and see if your rods change direction and point toward the healer's hands. With rods in hand, start backing away from the healer. When your rods stop pointing towards the healer, you are the periphery of their draw. Look at the floor and mark the spot and then measure that spot to the center of the healer's hands.

Otherwise begin with your dowsing rods over the healer's hands while he or she is doing an energy healing and see if you can dowse out the Earth Prana flowing towards them on the client. A radiant circle of Earth Prana flowing in from 360° degrees towards the healer's hands will form when the healing begins. Your rods should be pointing towards the healer's hands. Ask your rods to point directly against the flow of prana. Walk away from the healing. When your rods change direction you are at the edge of the healer's draw. Mark and measure it.

Next try standing ten to fifteen feet away from the healing, facing at a right angle (90°) to the healing. Ask to be shown the vortex of the healing. Your rods should point at a right angle towards the healing. Turn towards the healing. Your rods should be pointing straight ahead. Walk towards the healing. When your rods open up you are the periphery of the healer's draw. Mark and measure it.

As an additional exercise use your rods to trace out the periphery of the healer's draw. Find the edge of the healer's draw and ask your rods to trace it out. You should be walking out a circle around the healer.

Exhibit 6-5
Sensing or dowsing a vortex of Cosmic Prana

Finding a natural vortex of Cosmic Prana is much more difficult than finding a natural vortex of Earth Prana. I suggest getting comfortable finding vortices of Earth Prana (Exhibit 5-3) before tackling vortices of Cosmic Prana.

If you are a skilled dowser you should be able to learn how to find a vortex of Cosmic Prana with some time and effort. First, you need to find a place that has a vortex of Cosmic Prana. Simply going to a so-called *sacred site* may not be the place to begin. You need to go where serious meditating occurs, and/or loving acts of service and social justice regularly take place. I suggest a place where people who are not associated with major religions meditate daily for a few hours.

Spend time in prayer and reflection before beginning. As with looking for a natural vortex of Earth Prana, ask where the vortex of Cosmic Prana is located. If you are fortunate to have found one, follow the same instructions for finding a natural vortex of Earth Prana (Exhibit 5-3.) Spend some time in and around the vortex, taking several measurements, and try to get a feel for it. You should experience a positive, uplifting feeling in your chidakasha, your forehead area. I strongly suggest meditating and praying within the vortex as well as saying thanks.

You might try to get a sense for Cosmic Prana by dowsing the cushion, or the area where a dedicated meditator regularly meditates. This will help hone in your sense of Cosmic Prana.

Once you are able to find a vortex of Cosmic Prana, begin exploring hidden and out of the way places. Over time you will begin finding them as frequently as I did with my mountaintop meditation in Vermont.

Chapter 7

Negative Vortices

Tornadoes, Hurricanes

While a natural vortex with its positive geographic samskara can be uplifting and consciousness-raising, a negative vortex will deplete you and is detrimental to your health. It does not draw more prana into you but instead drains you of your prana. In doing so a negative vortex creates a host of problems and ailments from headaches to life-threatening diseases. Unfortunately negative vortices abound in the world.

When looking at negative vortices it is important to consider the microcosm and the macrocosm, the subtle body and Mother Earth and her planes of existence. Illnesses and violent storms, such as tornadoes, have the same underlying pattern, a counterclockwise spinning negative vortex.

Geographic samskaras and their vortices have a morality to them. Bad intentions such as selfishness and violence create negative samskaras that disturb the flow of prana. A disruption in the flow of prana has negative consequences for all of life and Mother Earth.

The Wrath

The idea that bad or negative behavior ravages Mother Earth and ultimately humankind is an old one. The bible teaches that our actions have consequences both for us and for Mother Earth, and ultimately bad behavior leads to hardship or worse. In a rather apocalyptic vision, Isaiah foretells how God will ravage the world: "Now the Lord is about to lay waste the earth and make it desolate, and he will twist its surface and scatter its inhabitants."[1] He goes on to say that Yahweh is doing this because our actions have polluted Mother Earth; "The earth lies polluted under its inhabitants; for they have transgressed laws, violated the statutes, broken the everlasting covenant."[2]

Similarly Ezekiel[3] and Jeremiah[4] teach us that famine and pestilence are the result of living outside of God's law. Amos[5] educates that the consequences of ignoring the Sabbath, of being dishonest, or taking advantage of the poor by selling them for a pair of sandals, or denying the poor the sweepings of wheat, will make the land tremble and the sun go down in broad day light. These comments conjure up images of a God of wrath, rather than an informative God who is teaching us about the concept of karma, that our actions have consequences, as well as how our behavior affects Mother Earth and in doing so affects us. The voice, or the way that the prophet tells us this makes God seem vindictive and hateful. It appears that God is not a God of love.

I have been rebuked on several occasions when I have brought up how our thinking and behavior damages Mother Earth, and how a damaged Mother Earth brings about calamity. Certain areas of Mother Earth are very much damaged. My comments have been perceived as being judgmental.

God speaks to each age in a voice that will be understood. We need to see the impact our consciousness has upon Mother Earth and ultimately upon ourselves. God's comments through the prophets still rings true today, and we should not judge their intention and delivery by our modern day standards. Do not look at the garb adorning it in the form of delivery, but rather at the underlying truth or intent. The fact is there is karma associated with violence, the abuse of the poor, materialism and selfishness. It is both an individual and collective karma that is intertwined with both humankind and Mother Earth.

The Macrocosm Formation Process

Negative energy vortices begin as negative land imprints that have a counterclockwise spin (clockwise in the southern hemisphere.) Their pattern of development is similar to that of positive energy vortices, only they form where bad things such as violence, hate, thievery or negative thinking have occurred. Negative land imprints disrupt the flow of prana in comparison to positive land imprints that enhance the flow of prana.

A negative land imprint grows by pulling people into its web of negative thinking and behavior, such as violence or selfishness. This repetitive pattern of thinking or action provides nourishment; thought is power, and the negative land imprint gets stronger when we succumb to it. Initially when they form, there is only a slight if any influence upon the flow of Earth Prana. As it grows it will begin to disrupt the flow of prana, meaning that prana within the area of the negative land imprint is interrupted and does not move smoothly in a straight manner towards an Earth Chakra.

When the movement of prana is disturbed by a negative land imprint Mother Earth's field, or grid is compromised. This means anyone within that area is not getting the full dose of prana they are supposed to get. Your energy body is meant to be immersed in prana 24/7.

At some point a major blockage in the flow of prana will develop if the negative land imprint is fed enough negative thoughts and behavior. A blockage is a pre-negative vortex formation that develops just prior to the formation of vortex. When a blockage occurs, the flow of Earth Prana is totally blocked in that particular area. This creates a dead spot where you are totally deprived of Earth Prana. Compare this to a natural vortex which is preceded by a circular pattern in the movement of prana (vortex ring.)

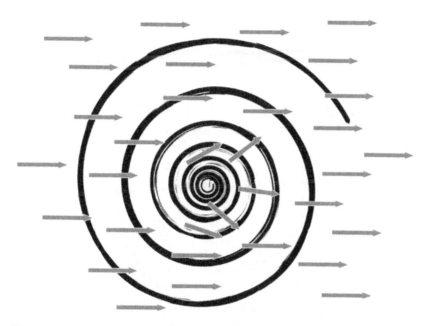

Exhibit 7-1a. Formation of a negative energy vortex begins with a negative land imprint. Notice how the flow of prana is disrupted in the center of the land imprint away from the center.

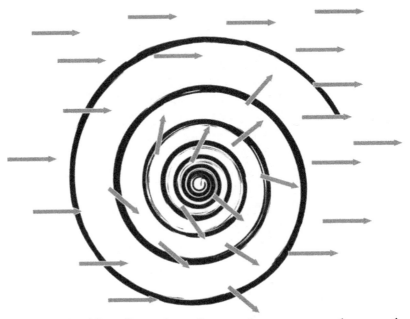

Exhibit 7-1b. The dispersion of prana increases, as the negative land imprint gets stronger.

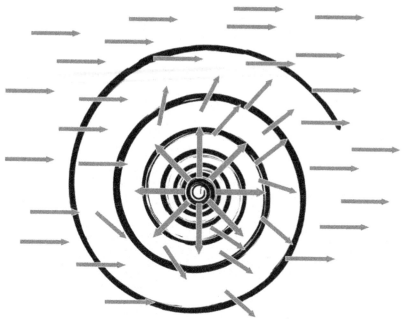

Exhibit 7-1c. A negative energy vortex forms. In the center of the negative land imprint prana explodes out, all the prana within the negative land imprint is affected.

The energy flow of a negative vortex follows a pattern similar to that of an explosion as described by Viktor Schauberger. A negative energy vortex drains you of your prana, drawing it into its center and then exploding out (Exhibit 7-2.) This is opposite to a natural vortex that pulls prana from the Energy Plane into its center and then funnels it through you. Basically a positive energy vortex feeds you and a negative vortex drains you.

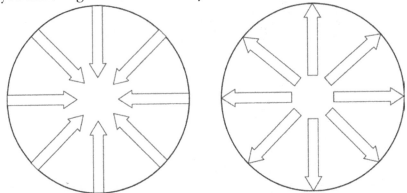

Exhibit 7-2. Implosion/Explosion, differences in the flow of prana. The drawing on the left is a positive energy vortex that pulls prana into you. While, the drawing on the right is of a negative energy vortex that drains you of your prana.

Negative energy vortices are one of the biggest components of geopathic stress, creating innumerable diseases from migraines to sleep disorders and worse with long-term exposure.

The reach of a negative vortex can be far beyond its spinning vortex. I can feel the affect of a negative vortex quite a distance from it, anywhere from a few feet to much more. This is partly because the flow of prana is disrupted around the vortex. Clearly a negative energy vortex has ramifications beyond its vortex.

Some Observations

Based upon my study of negative energy vortices, it appears they begin by initially draining you of Earth Prana, or lower consciousness component pranas. As the negative geographic samskara and its vortex continue to grow, they begin disrupting pranas with a higher consciousness component. This is opposite to a natural vortex that limits its affects to one type of prana and does not expand to include other pranas. I must admit I have not studied the growth process of negative vortices the way I have studied natural vortices. I have seen this pattern on a couple of occasions.

The idea that as a negative energy vortex grows, it begins to feed on other pranas with a higher consciousness component, which makes sense if you consider it is a deterioration process. This begins with the lowest fruit and grows by consuming higher forms of prana. Instead of the ascension process of purusha merging with prakriti, it is destroying the merger possibilities.

It also interesting to note that the movement of prana returns to its normal flow some distance after the negative energy vortex, on its way to an Earth Chakra. In other words the Earth Prana leaving a duct may at some point be blocked by a negative energy vortex, but will resume its normal path some time before it is pulled into the vortex of an Earth Chakra. So the flow of prana resembles water in a stream that is blocked at some point and then resumes its movement after the blockage.

Just as positive natural vortices can remain in existence for a long time, so too, can negative ones.

The Microcosm

The same pattern of formation for a negative energy vortex on Mother Earth's surface is found in the human subtle body. When prana is blocked that part of the body where the blockage is located does not get enough of the life force. This deprivation of nourishment eventually leads to disease.

Here is how psychotherapist and clairvoyant, Phoebe Bendit, and her husband, parapsychologist, Lawrence Bendit, describe the evolution of a negative vortex in the human subtle body:

> There is a slight break in the rhythm of the vital currents over the site of the injury… This is often visible long before there is any evidence of organic trouble. It begins as a batch of disorganization of the currents in the particular part of the field over the organ affected. The rhythmic flow becomes broken and irregular, and small vortices form in which, as in a river whirlpool, waste matter accumulates instead of being thrown out…The movement slows down until real stagnation occurs. Then, at a certain point, the whole process becomes, as it were, precipitated into the level of the physical tissues and local organic disease is established.[6]

In other words the blockage of prana and the development of a negative vortex in the human subtle body leads to disease, which may take a long time to manifest.

Types of Illnesses

A negative energy vortex blocks the flow of prana and drains you of prana. It is an explosive, destructive, disintegrating and decaying pattern or movement, occurring to those who come within its vortex. Studies of animals deprived of Mother Earth's energy field, through the shielding of the geomagnetic field, showed atypical growth of cells and tissues, changes to the morphology and functioning of internal organs, and premature death; while microorganisms similarly deprived produced mutant cell growth.[7]

Dr. Robert Gerber in his book *Vibrational Medicine* notes "the blood of normal individuals had a subtle energetic quality associated with the clockwise rotation of polarity….[I]ndividuals living in regions associated with geopathic stress tended to have a counterclockwise rotational polarity in their blood."[8] In other words, the polarity of the flow of blood for those living in areas of geopathic stress, where the environment or Mother Earth was damaged, had the same counterclockwise movement as that of a negative energy vortex, or negative geographic samskara. Fortunately, Gerber noted that once someone moved from an area of geopathic stress to a healthy environment, his or her blood returned to its normal clockwise movement.

According to Gerber, researchers have found the majority of patients with cancer had a counterclockwise polarity in their blood. He also noted "individuals with this abnormal polarity who are ill are usually resistant to any form of subtle energetic or vibrational medicine intervention."[9] This is sad but it shows how draining a negative vortex can be. I can tell you firsthand it is incredibility difficult to clear and remove a negative energy vortex from a space.

The Macrocosm

Like us, Mother Earth is ravaged by a variety of negative vortices. The larger ones are well known, such as tornadoes, hurricanes and typhoons, and are all very visible and incredibly destructive. All of these violent storms have a counterclockwise (clockwise in the southern hemisphere) spin.

Science tells us that hurricanes and tornadoes begin as violent thunder or rain storms that grow with the convergence of an updraft of warm air, from the surface of the Earth, meeting a cold air downdraft, creating a funnel. The Coriolis Effect causes the funnel to rotate.

The few times I studied areas where tornadoes landed, I found they manifested within the area of a very, very large negative geographic samskara. As I noted earlier geographic samskaras come in many sizes and can have both positive and negative components.

There are also clusters within clusters. Apparently, the paths where tornadoes touch down are in the more negative areas within a larger negative geographic samskara. Again, the population I have examined is small and negative geographic samskaras abound around the world, so to say some place is negative would not be a very differentiating factor.

Geopathic Stress

Hippocrates, the father of western medicine, said, "Illnesses do not come upon us out of the blue. They are developed from small deadly sins against nature. When enough sins have accumulated, illness will suddenly appear."[10] Those words ring even more than they did in the fifth century BC.

When we damage Mother Earth we are damaging ourselves. Our energy body needs energy to properly function lest we get sick. Even slight deviations can cause problems. Geopathic stress has been traditionally defined as an area where energies within the Earth have been disturbed or disrupted, thereby damaging the Earth's grid and releasing harmful energies.

A broader definition of geopathic stress should include areas covered with negative geographic samskaras, particularly areas with negative energy vortices. These are areas that can make you feel sick and bring about illness. Whether someone gets sick will be a function of his or her sensitivity to geographic samskaras, how bad the damage is to Mother Earth at the location, and the time spent in the area, as well as other factors.

Geomancer David Cowan, who has dowsed just about all of Scotland in search of Ley lines and written a book about the subject,[11] has found what he calls black spirals—a clockwise spinning vortex with a counterclockwise spiral imposed upon it. He describes them as malevolent and not conducive to health. Cowan believes we have created *artificial leys* (manmade ley lines) from radar, microwave towers, television stations and other technologies. Once these come in contact with other manmade disturbances below the surface of the Earth, such, as quarrying, drilling and the like, a black spiral forms which begins to draw in telluric currents, energy in the surface of the Earth that feed it.

Sick Houses

Cancer houses and sick houses are homes that make you sick. In 1929 Gustav Freiherr von Pohl felt that the high incidence of cancer in his hometown of Vilsbiburg, in southern Germany, was caused by detrimental Earth energies. Of the 565 houses and 900 apartments in town, forty-two of the houses had seven cancer deaths. He found these houses were in areas that had what he described as detrimental Earth energies.[12]

A few years back I briefly worked for a company that had an office with several negative energy vortices within it. The surrounding area was similarly damaged. Whenever I went there I got a splitting headache, a very drained and debilitating feeling, as well as feeling as though my subtle body had been placed in a washer and was being tumbled around. I was not alone. Several people complained about migraines. Two people in particular, who were the closest to two of the negative energy vortices, had been experiencing severe migraines. The migraines were so severe they sought medical help for a cure. No disease or cure was found.

Should you ever get migraines or any serious disease you should check to see if it you are in contact with a negative energy vortex, or an area of geopathic stress, before undergoing any dramatic procedure.

Symptoms of a Negative Vortex

Negative energy vortices are draining and debilitating. How they affect and are felt by individuals varies. You may feel a pinching in your forehead area and a drain or pain in your ajna chakra (between your eyebrows.) You may also get a draining feeling as if your blood sugar dropped quickly and you feel very weak.

Headaches and migraines are the immediate results of being in a negative vortex. You may also experience pre-migraine symptoms such as what I call seeing "fuzzies," or what medicine calls seeing an aura; your vision is impaired.

A variety of illnesses, from cancer to diseases associated with a compromised immune system or inflammation, can result if you spend too much time in a negative energy vortex.

Negative energy vortices will affect their immediate environment. If you see gnarled, twisted and deformed trees, there is a good chance it is an area of geopathic stress and a negative energy vortex could be causing stress to the environment.

Violent and Selfish Behavior

We are told that negativity, whether it be in our thinking or in our behavior, is bad for our health. Negative vortices demonstrate how damaging negativity can be.

Violent and selfish behavior damages our human subtle body, Mother Earth and her grid. The result of which is illness and even death. Damages to Mother Earth affect everyone, so what your neighbor does can have an impact on you. Act selflessly, give, heal, pray, mediate and be part of the cure--not the problem.

Exhibit 7-3
Dowsing Negative Energy Vortices

While holding your L-rods ask Spirit to show you where a negative energy vortex is located. Follow the direction the L-rods are pointing. My rods go to the vortex and then begin spinning counterclockwise within the vortex. Depending upon your preferences your rods may open up or go to one side. The speed of the spin will be one barometer of its strength. You may also wish to see what type of prana is being sucked into the negative energy vortex.

Chapter 8

Creating Vortices

Getting a vortex to form is no easy feat. However, there are several things you can do to enhance your efforts. Understanding the formation process and technique are helpful, but ultimately it depends upon you, your spiritual acumen, your sentience of Mother Earth and your perseverance. Approach your Mother with love, sincerity and the best of intentions.

Vortices form in response to human intentions. Your focus or activity will attract a specific type of prana or pranas. So your intention will dictate what type of energy vortex you will create.

A Natural Formation

It is not necessary to take specific steps to create an energy vortex, although it significantly helps. They form naturally where particularly positive intentions or actions have occurred for an extended period of time. Vortices of Earth Prana form all the time at locations where healing takes place. Vortices of Cosmic Prana form naturally where good thoughts and actions and focus on the divine take place regularly.

A few years back I returned to New York City, where I had lived for over two decades, and visited my astrologer friend, Bill Attride,[1] who had been very helpful years earlier in guiding me during my transformation from Wall Street money manager to my spiritual path. He was one of my first teachers and introduced me to

Theosophy and the ancient teachings. When I sat down on his couch I felt a very uplifting sensation. This was the couch where Bill's clients sat during their readings.

When I took out my dowsing rods I found a vortex of Cosmic Prana was beginning to form; there was a strong circling pattern of Cosmic Prana (vortex rings) and a vortex seemed imminent. This circulating formation of Cosmic Prana was located about midway between Bill's chair and the couch where his clients sat.

Bill's intentions were helping bring about this pre-vortex formation. He sees his astrological work as an effort to educate and help people along in their spiritual path. He is always instructing on the life's lessons one is supposed to learn at a particular juncture of his or her life. He is not focused on money or materialistic things, but rather on growth and spiritual development. It is this intention of service, compassion and growth that was driving the vortex's formation.

Again, it was the intention behind the astrology reading that was creating the vortex ring of Cosmic Prana. Had Bill's focus been on material gain, there would be no vortex ring, and it may well have been that a negative geographic samskara would have formed. Intention is the key.

The Formation Process

The formation of a vortex begins with a geographic samskara. Without a strong foundation, a strong positive geographic samskara, one focused on your intention and purpose, a vortex will not form. So when you are seeking to create a vortex you should concentrate on the geographic samskara first and foremost.

Spend some time contemplating what you are hoping to accomplish. Ponder it and do some research. The more you focus on it, the stronger the thought form becomes.

Honor Mother Earth

Honoring Mother Earth, particularly at the location where you want your vortex to form, will be a big help and can overcome handicaps. A vortex is a co-creation with Mother Earth so you need to have a good relationship with Her. Honor Her. Love Her.

Make your space holy and treat it accordingly. Have a ceremony to initiate your effort. Keep it pure by not harboring an evil thought when in close proximity to your chosen location. Honor it with flowers and a daily prayer. Give thanks to Mother Earth there.

Consider smudging the space particularly if you think it has been violated.

Keep the space secluded from other activities and people. Again you are looking to create a geographic samskara. Concentration and focus on one thought, healing, or prayer, will help in the formation process. Other activities in close proximity are distractions that will hamper your efforts. Similarly, visitors focused on other things besides your designed intention will detract from your effort. However, several people devoted to your intention, for example doing group healings or group prayers can be very helpful and is recommended.

Honor your space, love it and be devoted to it and Mother Earth.

Influencing Factors

Many factors will have influence on how long it takes to form a vortex or whether you can even get one to form.

Sentience of Mother Earth—Focusing on Mother Earth's blessing of energy to you will help. To know Mother Earth is to be able to feel and sense Her. Gaining sentience of Mother Earth is a good thing that we should all strive for, and has innumerable health benefits to hasten your spiritual advance. You can facilitate this process by trying to sense Her.

When conducting your activity (healing, praying, or meditating) occasionally begin to focus on the sensations coming to you. Feel the prana coming into you from Mother Earth. Focusing on those nascent feelings will give strength to them and increase your draw of prana. A larger draw means you are creating a larger imprint on the space, which means you are having a larger influence upon your space.

You can also visualize your co-creation with Mother Earth. See Her showering you with prana. See yourself working with Her to form a vortex. See a vortex forming in your chosen location.

By focusing on the flow of prana, you are emphasizing the samskara of the vortex you wish to create. This emphasis will give strength to the vortex and the flow of prana. However, the bulk of your time should be spent on your specific intention and activity.

Spiritual or Healing Ability—Being devout and maintaining a rigorous program of spiritual exercises helps with making a positive geographic samskara. Just as an athlete needs to develop physical strength and stamina, so does the spiritual aspirant need to develop his or her spiritual self. Meditation is a great way to strengthen your spiritual self.

Intention—The purer your intention--love, help and sincerity-- the better.

Perseverance—Effort and hard work are needed. You need to spend time and effort in the space where you wish the vortex to form; lots and lots of time. It may take years for your vortex to form, if it will ever form.

Type of prana—Making a vortex of Earth Prana is easier than making a vortex of Cosmic Prana.

Choosing Your Location

You can work with Mother Earth to build a vortex wherever you want. Preferably it is a secluded area that does not have a lot of traffic or other influences to hamper your effort. If you do not have a secluded location, make sure the space you decide upon is dedicated to your effort.

The space you choose has its own history contained in its geographic samskaras. It also has linkages to those who own the property or are in some other way connected to the property. Property owned by institutions can be tricky, because institutions are collective thought forms, independent entities that reflect the intentions and consciousness of its members past and present. If this includes the destruction of Mother Earth, or those devoted to Her, then it may be wearing an albatross that is too big for you to overcome.

I would avoid the property of major religions or corporations because it is challenging, if not impossible, to get vortices to form there. To many this might sound unimaginable, a heresy, that religious property may be unfruitful, after all it is a place of worship where people pray and is supposed to be a holy and sacred place. Experience teaches me otherwise.

For years I have been searching for and surveying sacred sites. I was often surprised when certain places that had divine aspects of Mother Earth, where people prayed, did not have vortices. Some of these places did not even have the sensation that people prayed there. Places where very devout people pray usually have a palpable feel to them, a powerful geographic samskara.

Only recently did I conclude that religious affiliations can hamper the formation of a vortex. This is because an institution's space carries the institution's collective consciousness, and it is that consciousness hindering the space.

Similarly, unaffiliated or smaller religious organizations focused on money, concerned more about membership and structure rather than service and the divine, or under a controlling leader, will cast a pallor on a location. Gurus are also very problematic. They bring the worship of an individual, power and often money. Remember Krishanmurti's words, "Truth is a pathless land. Man cannot come to it through any organization, through any creed, through any dogma, priest or ritual, nor through any philosophical knowledge or psychological technique."[2] Organizations are collective thought forms we have given life to. They are about control, putting forth a particular belief, or selling a particular product. This is not positive consciousness.

Unity—You are a Reflection of Your Circles

You are a sum total of all your relationships. Just as institutional property is a reflection of its members and history, you are a sum of all your friends, family, groups, clubs, work affiliations, religious organizations, institutions, corporations and the like, as well as objects you own such as technology and automobiles. Each relationship you have is a circle that seeks to bring together its members. You are united to these circles through your intention rather than by your location, as is the case with a land imprint. Each circle looks to merge with your consciousness and shape you, as well as being shaped by you.

Some years back I began a very aggressive meditative practice to achieve the meditative state of Samadhi. I emphasized the Hindu practice of meditating on an object, instead of focusing on my breath or stilling my mind by emptying it of all thoughts.

It is said that when you focus on an object you will eventually merge with it and in doing so the object will reveal itself to you. As I progressed deeper into my mediation on the object I began to get insights about it. I also began to realize that my consciousness quotient was increasingly being influenced by the object's consciousness reading more and more. While the object was a lovely flower, it had been adored and cultivated throughout history by people with materialistic purposes. It is said you should never change your object of meditation; however, after some contemplation I did. I chose a divine image, a prayer, and request given to me by God years earlier. A few years later God blessed me with some divine meditative states.

Whether you are looking to make a vortex, or develop your spiritual self, your unity circles will influence your effort. How much will depend upon the strength of the relationship, the strength of the circle, your devotion to the circle and more. As they say, choose your friends, or in this case, choose your circle of friends carefully; the Law of Unity looks to unite your consciousness and thinking with the many circles in your life.

This is not to say avoid bad or evil people. The Law of Unity is much more nuanced. If you follow the path of service and are looking to help others who may not have the highest of morals, you will be garnering other benefits that will exceed any detriments you may get by making circles with such people.

Technology Kills

Try and keep technology out of the area where you wish to co-create a vortex with Mother Earth. Modern technology is destructive and an anathema to Mother Earth.[3]

Dr. Robert Becker, twice nominated for the Nobel Prize for his pioneering work with bioelectrical magnetism and tissue regeneration, was a staunch critic of telecommunication. Through his research he came to realize all living organisms have a magnetic field surrounding them, intimately connected to and influenced by the Earth's geomagnetic field. Further, minute changes in the geomagnetic field could have significant influences upon life. It became clear to Dr. Becker that all of methods of communication, from radio waves, to cell phones and transmission services—such as electric power lines—disturbed the geomagnetic field and were a threat to life.

Dr. Becker wrote, "the exposure of living organisms to abnormal electromagnetic fields results in significant abnormalities in physiology and function."[4] He believed the greatest discovery of the twentieth century was the knowledge of the geomagnetic field as a significant environmental variable upon the fields of life, comparable to William Gilbert's launch of the scientific revolution in 1600. Dr. Becker felt this knowledge was the key to understanding the risks of technology as well as opening up a new world of possibilities.[5]

Technology is a particularly pernicious consciousness that is incredibly detrimental to Mother Earth. It is one of death and destruction, as Schauberger taught. Technology wreaks havoc on Mother Earth and humankind's subtle body. All of our electronic and digital devices disturb the Pranic Plane and can emanate their own detrimental fields. We are microwaving Mother Earth to death.

If you want a vortex to form you need to reduce the amount of technology in your life. Consider getting rid of your cell phone and limit your computers, tablets and other digital devices. Go retro and use older technologies as much as possible—the older the better; read real books not tablets. Hydrocarbons are incredibly damaging to Mother Earth, but what is far more damaging are electronic devices that break up Her field and reduce Her ability to respond to other problems such as pollution. Think of it this way, if pollution were a raging fire then technology would be the villain that cuts the fire hose and prevents the fire from being extinguished.

Negative Talismans

Not only is a space a reflection of the thoughts that take place within its circle, but it is also a reflection of the consciousness of the objects within it. You may have divine thoughts within a space, but if it is filled with negative talismans they will dampen your effort.

In a sea of consciousness, everything has consciousness—even inanimate objects. All objects are a reflection of the consciousness that made them, the underlying materials as well as thoughts and intentions that constructed them. Objects also pick up the consciousness and thoughts of all those they come in contact with. So when you bring something into your life or home you are bringing in the sum of all that is behind the object. When you keep that object in your home or close to your chosen location to form a vortex, that consciousness is there 24-7.

You need to be cognizant of the talismans you have in your home and in your chosen location. Do not own violent talismans such as guns, and choose natural materials not synthetics. Bring the divine and natural objects into your vortex area.

Where Will It Form

So you have selected a location. Where will the vortex form? A vortex will form wherever healing, spiritual practices and good deeds take place.

Generally, the rough rule of thumb is if you pray, or mediate, or do healings consistently in the same place the vortex will form in that exact location. The location can be influenced by other factors, such a nearby divine aspect of Mother Earth that may exert some pull towards it.

Vortices also form from group activities. Where they form will be a composite of those who helped create the vortex. For example, if there are two people driving the formation process, then the

105

vortex will most likely form midway between them as was the case with my astrologer friend, Bill, and his clients. If we increase the number of people meditating or praying, then the vortex will form in some central location to them. A variety of factors will influence where a vortex forms: the spiritual acumen of the participants, as well as time/effort spent by them at the location. See Exhibit 8-1.

Mother Earth Can Override

Location can influence the type of vortex that forms at a particular place. Actions done on a specific aspect of Mother Earth may form a vortex of that divine aspect, rather than a vortex of the prana you would normally attract based upon intentions.

I have found prayer and meditation done in a Field of Consciousness,[6] an aspect of Mother Earth's soul, in greater upstate New York[7] will form a unique type of vortex. Ley lines, or lines of consciousness, which many associate with sacred sites, originate from these fields. The fields charge up the ley lines with consciousness, which they then carry to distant corners of the world. Fields of Consciousness are incredibly powerful. Some of the people who have lived in close proximity to Fields of Consciousness have helped shape our collective psyche from leaders in the women's movement, to the abolitionist movement, to America's Second Great Awakening.[8]

When you meditate, pray, or do ceremony within such a Field, a vortex can form. The vortex will be made up of the consciousness emanating from the Field. Interestingly, such a vortex appears to have minimal bearing on the flow of Cosmic Prana which is what we usually attract when we do spiritual exercises.

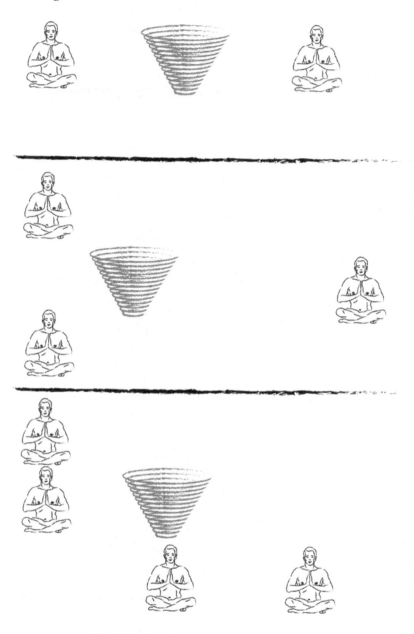

Exhibit 8-1. Where a Vortex will form.

A vortex on an aspect of Mother Earth may not have a whirlpool-like pattern to it. It may dowse out a whirlpool but something else might be going on. For example, a Field of Consciousness emanates consciousness in a 360° pattern to nourish the ley lines that pass over them. When a vortex forms in a field, part of the emanation radiating out from it returns back in a 360° about-face. In other words, some of the emanation boomerangs back and returns after emanating out a short distance. Vortex may not be the right word to call such a formation. See Exhibit 8-2.

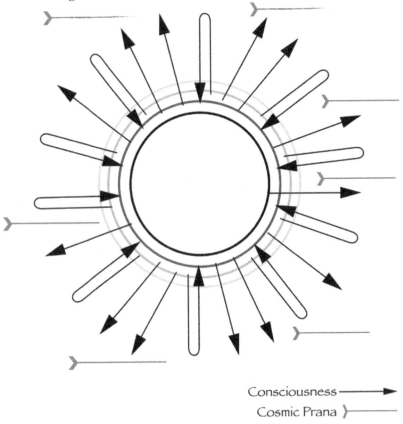

Consciousness ⟶

Cosmic Prana ⟩———

Exhibit 8-2. Vortex in a Field of Consciousness.

In Exhibit 8-2 consciousness is emanating, radiating out 360° from the circle in the center. Notice that some of the consciousness is returning back; or at least that is what appears to be happening. This raises several questions such as does this diminish the amount of consciousness emanating from that location, thereby reducing the amount of consciousness available for ley lines to pick up before they begin their global journey? NO! The vortex significantly enhances the production of consciousness. Just as the union of human kind with Mother Earth to create an energy vortex enhances the flow of prana so does such a union in a Field of Consciousness enhance the flow of consciousness. I can tell you first-hand I was able to sense and learn about Fields of Consciousness because I was able to sense a vortex within it and began meditating in it. Initially I could not sense or feel the rest of the field.

Notice in Exhibit 8-2 there is no influence on the flow of Cosmic Prana that would usually be attracted to activities such as prayer, ritual or meditation that created this vortex. I cannot say why this is; I can only assume that it might be because aspects of Mother Earth override, or that the essence with the highest consciousness component trump out.

Creating Talismans

A vortex will also attach to nearby objects where you wish your vortex to form. For example, a vortex will form on a nearby meditation cushion or on a healers' table.

Everything within the draw of the person performing the activity will form a vortex. For example, if you have a draw of two feet in radius when meditating, then everything within a two foot radius of you that is there consistently, such as your meditation cushion, a rug, a chair and even knick knacks, will have a vortex form and attach to them.

It is important to note that Mother Earth by herself cannot activate or charge anything. It takes a joint effort between Mother Earth and humankind to charge a stone. If you leave a stone or object on a divine aspect of Mother Earth, it will not be impacted at all. The object will only be charged or form a vortex when it comes in contact with human consciousness.

Instead of having a small stack of stones next to you, use the stones to create a circle, thereby they will perform two functions. Make sure that the circle does not extend beyond your draw. A bag of stones is fine as well.

The size of your talisman does not matter. I have used stones less than 1/2 inch in width for talisman that have had vortices two feet or more in radius form on them.

The draw of prana of a talisman's vortex, like all vortices, will grow in size over time, as long as its geographic samskara is fed and reinforced with its underlying thoughts and consciousness.

When you bring a talisman into contact with a conflicting geographic samskara in another area, the vortex will begin to diminish in size and strength. However, it will begin to influence the space it is within. The vortex may disappear over time if it is kept in a conflicting area.

Stone Circles

One of the things I love to do is work with stones to create structures to enhance a space and work with Mother Earth. I feel blessed to have been able to tap into the consciousness and knowledge of an ancient group I call Spirit Keepers.[9] I have found what I believe to be the remnants of their stone work in Fields of Consciousness in upstate New York. They have taught me a lot about the ancient art of working with stones and much, much more.

One of the oldest, most popular and easiest structures to create is a stone circle. The circle is also one of the most important, particularly when it comes to making vortices. A stone circle will facilitate the creation of a vortex, and to me this is one of the primary purposes of a stone circle. There are a host of other uses and purposes for making stone circles.

Religious historian, Mircea Eliade, said that a circle of stones and similar walled enclosures are "the most ancient forms of man-made sanctuary."[10] They were meant to separate the sacred from the profane of everyday life, providing a *centre*[11] in a turbulent world. According to Eliade, city walls were erected for sanctuary long before they served as military erections. Similarly, by creating a stone circle, you are defining your sacred space.

A circle mimics the shape of a samskara and its vortex. You are also giving concrete form to your intention as well as making a statement saying this is a sacred space, a special space. The stones will help retain and give shape to your intentions. The stone circle will help keep you focused and each time you look at it or think about it your thoughts will give strength to the place.

Small Is Better

I would recommend making a small stone circle, about twenty inches in diameter to a maximum two feet in diameter. Make the circle big enough to get the core of your body, particularly your spinal column to fit within it when you are sitting in a meditative pose.

It took some time for me to conclude that a stone circle should be small. For years I found the remnants of old Spirit Keeper stone circles that were not more than two feet in width, often about eighteen inches in diameter. Over time I began to notice some of these circles contained very strong natural vortices. Or I found a natural vortex that was quite small, but very palpable to feel, giving me a jolt when I came in contact with it. Eventually I realized they were designed to be small in diameter. My opinion about this and stone circles overall continues to evolve.

It appears that a smaller vortex, if designed to be smaller, is stronger, and more palpable to the senses than it would be if the same amount of effort were applied to a larger circle allowed to form unimpeded. I have no proof that a smaller vortex is better or draws in more prana—this is only a hypothesis, or observation, I need to investigate further.

Although stones block the flow of Earth Prana immediately about them, they do not block the flow of Cosmic Prana. It appears that your intentions to build a stone circle, a closure, limit or hamper the growth in size of the geographic samskara to the space within the stone circle.

Circles within Circles

This is not to say that you should only make small stone circles, but rather small stone circles will make a stronger vortex and may even hasten its formation.

There are a myriad of different types of circles you can make. Circles within circles, circles linked by sharing a common space, and on. Let's say you want to create a large circle where people can gather, with enough space to move around to do yoga exercises, but you also wish to have a vortex form within it. Make a larger stone circle and another smaller stone circle within it. The larger circle will serve the intentions of your overall purpose, and the smaller stone circle will hasten the creation of a vortex within it.

I would also avoid making large megaliths or stone structures that cannot be easily deconstructed or moved. Just as revelation is part of the spiritual experience, so it is with your relationship with Mother Earth. As you work with Mother Earth to improve and create sacred space, she will begin to reveal more of herself to you.

In the process, new areas of your space may become more appealing, and at the same time your sentience of Mother Earth will improve. This may change your preferences and understanding of Mother Earth, as well as where you want your stone circle to be located.

Make smaller, simpler structures. Go nuts with your intention and devotion. Small is beautiful.

Vortices within Vortices

One of the structures you may wish to consider making is three small stone circles surrounded by a larger stone circle. I have found similar formations at sacred spaces in upstate New York. Not actual stone structures, but a trio of vortices that I imagine were once stone circles.

When you make a trio of three small stone circles next to each other, and encompass them in a larger circle that surrounds them, over time and with effort each of them will form a vortex. A vortex may also form within the larger circle as an overlay vortex over the other three. This takes time and a lot of prayer and meditation to accomplish.

When I have done this with larger circles, the results have been not as good, or rather, I am still 1 working on them. Vortices formed within the centers of the three smaller circles which are six to eight feet in diameter each; but they were a fraction of the size of their individual circles. A circling pattern, or a quasi vortex ring, had formed within the periphery of the larger circle that encompassed the three smaller circles. Arguably the vortices may expand over time, covering all of their space and a larger overlay vortex encompassing all of the circles may form. But this would take a very, very long time, if ever. See Exhibit 8-3.

The key is to keep it small.

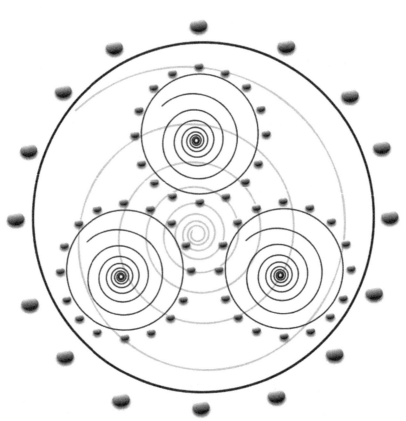

Exhibit 8-3. Trio of Stone Circles surrounded by a larger stone circle. Notice how vortices have formed in the smaller stone circle as well as in the center of the larger circle which surrounds them.

Empty Circle Technique

You don't have to meditate in a stone circle to have a vortex form within it. One of the techniques I have successfully used to create a vortex is to build a stone circle and meditate around it—not within it.

As I mentioned earlier it is not necessary to pray at a specific place to have a vortex form in the area. In places of worship, where people pray or meditate in various areas, a vortex will form in the center, based upon the weighted average of the group, their spiritual acumen, their time spent, and their distance from others. The empty circle technique uses this principle.

Years ago I was taught the empty circle technique at a very special place, within a very sacred place, where many things have been revealed to me. I was guided to build a stone circle about three to four feet in diameter. I was instructed not to pray or meditate within it. Instead I was guided to get a flat stone and to meditate on it at a location outside of the stone circle. Each time I visited the special place I would find a flat stone to meditate on outside of the circle. This went on for several years, and dozens and dozens of stones piled up around the circle, as did leaves, fallen tree branches, fauna and more. In fact the circle became almost indiscernible. Then one day I had the premonition to dowse the circle, and surprise—a vortex had formed within it. It was a vortex of something special and to this day I still do not know what it draws.

With the empty circle technique you pick the location where you wish the vortex to form. The formation process for the vortex is similar to that of a sacred space or place of worship where over time a vortex will form within it. You have to meditate around it at various locations not just on one side.

Infinite Possibilities

There are many more stone structures you can create. Just use your imagination and keep them small, or make them easy to dismantle when more is revealed to you and you move on.

Chapter 9

The Mystical Spiral Form

There is a mystical power or force to the vortex, its spiral form, and circular shape--something that the ancient peoples understood but has been lost over time. By mimicking the movement of the spiral they were tapping into that mystical power. Whether you imitate it through movement, or in physical displays in drawings, or just contemplate its form, you will be tapping into the power.

Old School

Ancient cultures incorporated the spiral form and movement into their rites and rituals. Jill Purce in her book, *The Mystic Spiral, Journey of the Soul*, describes how the Bavenda tribe of South Africa achieved 'cosmic harmony' and 'fertility' through the Deumba or python dance by identifying with the serpent force. The older women would gather in the center as the younger women would pivot and spiral inwards toward them.[1]

Similarly ancient pagan cultures imitated the spiral in their dances and rituals. Starhawk detailed the spiral dance in her book *Spiral Dance, A Rebirth of the Ancient Religion of the Goddess*. A line of dancers spirals clockwise into the center of a circle—the place of transformation and power—and then spiral out. The leader then spirals inward again, all the time chanting and making the loop tighter, and in the process raising the energy.[2]

Ancient megaliths around the world, some more than ten thousand years old, are engraved with spirals. Flinders Petrie, a Victorian archaeologist, noted for developing systematic approaches to site surveys called the spiral "the main feature of primitive decoration, often elaborately involved."[3] Irish archaeologist, Michael Morris, felt the spiral and concentric circle were the dominant motif of megalithic art. Morris believed "the spiral may have expressed the concept of life-energy...of cosmic energy and life's rhythms with which early man was concerned."[4]

Building Blocks of Consciousness

To our modern way of thinking, the notion that pagan rituals, which mimicked the movement of the spiral in dance, and the image of a spiral—achieve anything is unimaginable. We are so grounded in materialism that the power of movement and symbolism is lost. How can they have power?

In a sea of consciousness, everything at its core is consciousness. In other words, an object is a reflection of consciousness, as movement is a reflection of consciousness, as is language, as is color, as is.... Everything is consciousness. That is not to say everything has a high consciousness quotient, but rather everything at its most elemental level, or true being is consciousness.

Consciousness has a circular shape and spiral form. Whenever we reflect on something, or come in contact with it in some way, we connect. The Unity Principle teaches when we have these types of connections we begin to merge with that consciousness. It becomes one of the many circles in our life.

So when we do a spiral dance, we begin to merge with the spiral form, just as we would merge with an object of reflection, or merge with the many other circles in our life through our interactions. The more time and more intensity we apply to a circle, the stronger its influence upon us becomes. At the same time more of its being is revealed to us and we begin to tap into its being or powers.

Form, Word, Meaning

The process of contemplative meditation on an object shows how focusing on movement is no different from focusing on a physical object. By meditating on an object, we are connecting to it and beginning to fuse with it—the Unity Principle. When we focus on an object, we can meditate on its form, its word, or its meaning. For example, if we meditate on a dog we can focus on the form or mental image of a dog, or the word 'dog', or the meaning of what a dog is. Most people, when they meditate, focus on all three, or bounce back and forth between the three. Mantra, or word, can only bring us to the first level of Samadhi and no further. To advance into the higher states of Samadhi we must be able to distinguish between the three and focus on only one of the aspects. This implies there is a hierarchy to form, word, and meaning.

Chapter Three of Patanjali's *Yoga Sutras*, *Vibhooti Pada*, deals with siddhis or spiritual gifts. He teaches that particular supernatural powers come to us by focusing[5] on certain forms and functions. For example, he teaches that a yogi can achieve invisibility[6] by contemplating the form of his body, or the yogi can achieve the strength of an elephant[7] by contemplating on an elephant's strength.

Similarly there is a power, a force, and a beauty that can be achieved when we reflect upon or mimic the form or movement of the spiral—something beyond what our modern day minds can comprehend.[8] Mircea Eliade wrote[9] that the spiral symbolized water and fertility to ancient peoples and it united all aspects of life. This implies the spiral held the power of life and was the thread connecting everything.

119

The Circle

So by focusing on the spiral form, whether through contemplation, by physically imitating it, or seeing it in everything or through the word 'spiral/vortex,' you will be connecting with it and tapping into it. By doing so you will be unlocking the spiral's mysteries.

The most elemental of these forms is the circle. As I mentioned in the previous chapter, the circle is the great unifier. We can tap into it through stone circles and similar structures.

Mother Earth at Work

Viktor Schauberger believed that water, like everything else in the universe, was alive and needed to be constantly reinvigorated and brought back to life. He felt water did this by doing its own spiral dance:

When rain falls, like distilled water, it is without life. It trickles down in spiraling motions around rocks beneath the ground, where it gradually meets a rising temperature, and begins at some point to percolate upwards again in a spiraling motion, gathering material ions and life force until it meets light."[10]

Water bubbling to the surface of Earth is called *primary water* by water dowsers and is thought to be alive. Primary water is energized, and in coming from the Earth it is purified, distilled and of higher quality.[11]

Implicit in Schauberger's quote is that the spiraling movement contributes to giving life to and purifying water. He also postulated that the vortex acted as a synthesizer of various energies to create material form. Energies would be pulled into a vortex's funnel and travel down until they become too coarse to be pulled any further, at which point materialization would take place.

The Pattern of Existence

All of life, all of existence has a circular form with a spiral whirlwind. When we see reality as such, much will be revealed to us.

Psychiatrist Carl Gustav Jung described our psychological development like the movement of a spiral: "the conscious process moves spiral-wise round a center gradually getting closer, while the characteristic of the center grew more and more distant. Or perhaps, we could put it another way and say that the center—itself unknowable—acts like a magnet..."[12] The pull of a magnet is like the whirlpool of a vortex.

At the same time the spiral is expansive and represents growth. As we grow we are expanding like a spiral, yet we remain in the same place in the expression of who we are. The mathematician Jacob Bernoulli (1654-1705) was so impassioned with this principle that he requested a figure of a logarithmic spiral, and the motto "Eadem mutata resurgo" (*Changed and yet the same, I rise again*), be engraved on his gravestone.

Tapping into the Spiral Form

Several have mimicked the form and movement of a vortex for use in their respective disciplines. Leonardo Da Vinci observed the spiral and vortex in nature and applied their properties of form in his work. He understood that the formation of a vortex in the heart was necessary to help circulate the blood. His helicopter design was a large spiral called an aerial crew.

Most of Da Vinci's art and architecture use the principle of the golden spiral, or golden ratio, to achieve perfect proportion which is pleasing to the eye. A golden spiral is a logarithmic spiral based upon the golden ratio that gets wider the further it moves away from the center. The golden ratio occurs when the rate of expansion stays at a constant rate of 1.618, or phi.[13] Italian mathematician, and Franciscan Friar, Fra Luca Bartolomeo de

Pacioli, is called the Father of Accounting for giving us double-entry bookkeeping. He wrote a book titled, *The Divine Ratio* on the golden ratio. Clearly he felt it represented God's hand at work.

Modern day historians and analysts have expanded the use of the golden ratio and its related Fibonacci sequence of numbers,[14] and see it as playing out in the trends and patterns of human behavior. In other words, our patterns of behavior, our preferences, our thinking, our emotions, basically everything we think and do as humans follows a golden ratio, or spiral-like pattern.

Ralph Nelson Elliot, a retired accountant who took up technical analysis of the stock market, using past price movements to predict future prices, developed the popular Elliot Wave Principle to forecast future prices. He said his system worked because "All human activities have three distinctive features—pattern, time and ratio—all of which observe the Fibonacci Summation Series."[15] Elliot Waves see stock price rises and declines following the Fibonacci sequence. Robert R. Prechter, Jr. a follower of the Elliot Wave Principle, believes the growth of all life from bacteria, to animal, to human can be plotted as a logarithmic spiral.[16]

Matthew Cross and Robert Friedman, in their book *The Divine Code of Da Vinci, Fibonacci, Einstein and You,*[17] point out that the divine ratio is the universal form found in nature, in structure, function and movement of everything in the universe. They argue the greatest minds in history achieved success by tapping into and employing the divine ratio in their work, and you can do the same. They feel we can unlock the power of the spiral by embracing it in all that we think and do.

Movement Should Marry Form

Whenever you are creating space, cleaning space, or cleaning your subtle body, try to mimic the movement of a vortex. This will help your efforts and keep you in harmony with Mother Earth. For example, when I smudge someone's subtle body I try to move my hands in a circular clockwise pattern. In doing so I merge my actions with my intentions. Similarly, when I am cleaning space with a smudge stick or even just with my hands, I move my hands in a circular clockwise pattern of motion.

When you do not marry movement with your intention, you will be undermining your efforts. Marry movement with form.

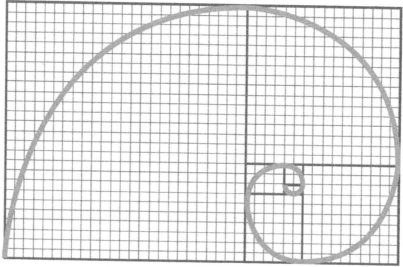

Exhibit 9-1. Logarithmic Spiral.

Labyrinths

The idea of working with stone is to create a structure that enhances Mother Earth and co-creates with Her a new birth or a new formation that benefits both. Many see labyrinths as a way of doing this. Unfortunately, a labyrinth, unless it has a spiral design, does not do this and actually harms Mother Earth's field and limits your ability to co-create with Her.

Many people who are passionate about Mother Earth are also passionate about labyrinths and see them as a way to connect with Her. But walking the twisted and constantly redirecting path of most labyrinths disrupts the flow of prana. Our subtle body leaves a human energy trail, a trail of consciousness and more wherever we go. Over time if we continue to walk on the same path, in the same direction, particularly if done with a focused or contemplative mind, that trail gets stronger and stronger. Eventually this trail begins to influence the flow of prana. If this path does not mimic a spiral, but instead has twists and turns that are constantly reversing and changing course, we create a hodgepodge of imprints that do not allow a vortex to form. In fact, such a path disrupts the flow of prana and disturbs Mother Earth and Her field.

Because the path is repeatedly walked with a contemplative mind, a vortex is not able to form. A clockwise spiraling path needs to be pursued in labyrinth-like structures if one wishes to have a vortex form. Such a path naturally replicates the clockwise movement of a vortex.

This is not to say that a labyrinth is not without benefits. All the contemplative thinking concentrated within a labyrinth can still create a strong geographic samskara of insight and inquiry. The insight that labyrinths have a design flaw came to me while walking a labyrinth at the Foundation of Light in Ithaca, New York.[18] As noted earlier, a labyrinth can attract water and create formations underground. So it still has benefits.

Labyrinths have been around for thousands of years and are much appreciated and used by many dedicated and well-intentioned people. Having people walk a clockwise spiral pathway inwards would facilitate the formation of a vortex. I believe the formation of a vortex within a spiral labyrinth would be a big boost to it, and would mark the beginning of more good things to come.[19]

You need to marry intention with form or movement if you wish to build a vortex. In Exhibit 9-2, I offer several alternatives to creating a labyrinth-like structure that would facilitate the creation of a vortex.

Exhibit 9-2
Possible Labyrinth-like configurations

Here are some alternative formations to create a labyrinth-like structure. I cannot attest to whether they work, but I do know it is nearly impossible to get a vortex to form within a traditional non-spiral labyrinth path.

Create a clockwise spiral path. Periodically check to see the movement of prana is not being restricted to the path. If so, periodically adjust the movement (width and tightness) of the spiral path until it blossoms into a vortex.

Create a large circle and a much smaller circle within it. The large circle with no path is where people can walk around in a contemplative mind. This will have people making their own path within the constraints of the stone circle. Make a smaller circle within the larger circle where you would like a vortex to form. You can have people pray/meditate/contemplate within it, but this is not necessary as a vortex should form over time regardless. This configuration employs an empty circle-like technique with the smaller circle acting as the empty circle.

Keep changing the path; you can try regularly altering the path so that a distinct path does not establish itself.

Again these are possible solutions I have not tested out. Experiment and keep readjusting.

Holes, Black Holes, Wi-Fi Holes

If mimicking a spiral can unlock its mysteries, then doing the exact opposite will manifest the hideous and debilitating properties of a negative energy vortex. When you mimic the movement of, or the form of a negative energy vortex, or dwell on it, or incorporate it into your life in other ways you will be tapping into it.

In the winter of 2010 I went to a mall outside of Buffalo, New York to give a talk on my recently released book, *The Way Home, Making Heaven on Earth*, and lead a group meditation. While I was setting up I got a strong pain in my head and felt a draining pull upon my subtle body. Thinking that I was detecting an area of geopathic stress, I took out my dowsing rods. They led me to a spot close by in the food court of the mall where I found a negative energy vortex. When I asked Larry Jackson of Light Bridges Magazine, the organizer of the event, about the space he mentioned that a lot of people used it as a Wi-Fi spot.

I don't know whether the Wi-Fi usage created the negative vortex. I also don't know much about the design and technology behind Wi-Fi, but I do know that the inventor of Wi-Fi mimicked the "science" of black hole for his design of Wi-Fi to get it work.[20] Black holes are a destructive force with gravity so strong even light is unable to escape. They exist in deep space and grow by absorbing the mass around them through their pull. Similarly a negative energy vortex drains you of prana.

The unfortunate thing is that the use of Wi-Fi is growing as more digital technology, automobiles, appliances and other technological devices are being linked up.

Be in Sync

There is a mystical power to the spiral form that underlies all of existence. Understand this and work with it. Try to incorporate the form and movement of a spiral into your life. See the pattern of life and human behavior playing out through the pattern of a spiral. Avoid mimicking the movement of a negative energy vortex or technological devices that do.

Similarly incorporate the circular form, a timeless symbol of unity and oneness, into your life. The Haudenosaunee[21] prophet, the Peacemaker, taught this when he brought together warring tribes to create the Iroquois Nation. It created a synergy far beyond the sum of its parts.

Since we do not know or cannot fully understand the reason ancient people mimicked the spiral form, one must wonder whether there is a greater force or power to the spiral and its circular shape.

Embrace it.

Chapter 10

Simple Things You Can Do with

Vortices

There are a variety of ways you can use vortices and you don't necessarily have to develop the ability to co-create one with Mother Earth. In fact, if you cannot create one, but can find one, it is a great device to help you improve your connection to Mother Earth and your meditative ability. I use vortices for a variety of purposes—such as protecting myself from detrimental energies, clearing space and for my work with sacred sites. They are a great tool!

Vortices can be used to heal you physically, mentally and spiritually. Talismans and intention circles are great tools, which healers and other practitioners can incorporate into their practice.

The Components

There are two main components to working with vortices, the samskara and the energy vortex. Whatever you are looking to accomplish, you need to understand how these components work because they are what will bring about change. How you use them will dictate the type of transformation you will achieve.

A samskara will try to influence the thinking of those who come within its circle. Its consciousness reading will either raise or lower the consciousness of anyone that comes within its circle.

The vortex brings an increased dose of energy, which has many benefits.

Intention Circles/Talismans

Intention circles are a great way to set the mood and tenor of a space. They are land imprints that reinforce a particular action, set the tone, cleanse and more. It is not necessary to have a vortex form for an intention circle, or talisman be useful. The formation of a vortex would be a barometer indicating you have reached a certain plateau.

For example, healers may wish to purify their clients before they begin a healing in order to remove negative thought forms or other spiritual debris. By creating a circle, talisman, or dedicated area where you do cleansings, you will be building up a powerful samskara by continually performing your cleansing there. Over time the samskara will get so strong that just having your client spend time within the space will help purify him them. As noted in Chapter 3, anesthetized mice recovered better in an area where other mice had previously recovered. Your cleansings will progressively get stronger as you perform them at the same location.

One of my favorite intention circles is to make, what I call a welcome circle, a stone circle that is meant to act like an entryway or foyer of a house. I primarily create welcome circles at sacred sites, but you can use them at other locations as well. For a sacred site I use welcome circles to prepare the visitor and spiritually cleanse him or her before entering the space. I do this with prayer whenever I am in the welcome circle. I give every visitor a warm and hearty greeting with a hug and read a prayer. Everyone is smudged in the welcome circle before entering the sacred space. Over time these actions create a powerful samskara focused on welcoming and cleansing.

You may wish to create a welcome circle close to your entryway so that anyone entering your home or office will walk through it when he or she enters your space. First impressions last a long time and you can help set the tone for what is to follow.

Having a positive vibe in your work and business area is important. When people feel good in a space, whether they know it consciously or not, they will want to spend time there. Intention circles and talismans can help you create a positive environment.

Similarly you can create intention circles for specific types of meditation. For example, I have different places where I do different types of meditations. One location is focused on cleansing and relaxation. Another place is where I introspect and look for answers. In my backyard there are a multitude of divine aspects of Mother Earth that I have placed stones on, or created a stone structure to enhance Her. At those places I do a variety of meditations but the primary focus is to tap into Mother Earth. Doing the same type of meditation at the same place will help develop a samskara for that type of meditation. Over time these areas can become very powerful. The chair in my living room where I do relaxation meditations has a vortex ten feet in radius and can put me into deep trance/sleep within minutes. You too can create such a spot for deep relaxation. Pick a location and focus strictly on relaxation and the removal of mental debris. Over time a powerful samskara will develop so that when trauma hits or you are very stressed you can go there and be better able to relax.

You can create an intention circle, or talisman, focused on any thought or emotion; happiness, laughter, communication...

Healing Talismans

Talismans are a great way to supplement healings. Make some talismans with vortices of Earth Prana by keeping them within the draw of your healings. Preferably use natural objects such as stones to avoid the unwanted consciousness underlying other objects, but objects such as pillows are fine.

Here are a few ideas on how to use them:

1. You can carry them with you to increase your draw when you do spontaneous healings away from your office.
2. Place them underneath your healing table at various locations to increase the draw of Earth Prana all over your client's body.
3. Give them to your clients

Linking You to Mother Earth

A talisman, or a natural vortex can better help you connect to Mother Earth. Such a connection can bring innumerable health and other benefits.

As noted earlier I first learned to sense and experience the sensation of consciousness within a vortex in a Field of Consciousness at a sacred site. The vortex increased the flow consciousness emanating from the field, making it more palpable to feel. The extra dose of consciousness helped me to experience it. I was also within a samskara made by some very accomplished spiritual aspirants who were devoted and connected to Mother Earth. Had I not encountered such a vortex it would have taken me longer to sense and experience consciousness.

Being connected to Mother Earth brings innumerable benefits. In *Earthing, The Most Important Health Discovery Ever?*[1] Clinton Ober, Stephen Sinatra (M.D.), and Martin Zucker explain that a strong connection to Mother Earth reduces inflammation, which is behind just about every chronic illness from heart disease, to cancer to rheumatic illnesses.[2] They recommend walking barefoot or sitting on an Earthing pad connected to Mother Earth to get a healthy dose of Her.

The *Earthing* authors feel that one of the factors missing in the cause of inflammation is "the lost connection to our planet's natural flow of surface electrical energy and the electron deficiency in our bodies that this creates. Our investigations strongly suggest the incidence of soaring chronic diseases during our lifetimes has occurred during a period in which more and more people have become increasingly disconnected from the Earth."[3] They believe that the flow of negatively charged electrons from the Earth into the body snuff out the free radicals that are behind inflammation.

According to the authors one of the other benefits of grounding is that it powerfully reduces electromagnetic fields (EMF's) on the body.[4] In other words a good connection to Mother Earth can help reduce your absorption of damaging EMF's compared to the average person. A prayer stone or talisman made by someone who had a strong bond with Mother Earth would improve your ability to connect with Her. By working with such a talisman you are working with their intentions and connections to Mother Earth.

Revitalizing Mother Earth's Field

Talismans, or prayer stones, can be used to help revitalize Mother Earth's field and get the flow of prana moving again. Negative geographic samskaras cause disruptions in the flow of prana, which can be severe. When you place a talisman in the area it will help restore the flow of prana. I generally use prayer stones for this, which are stone talismans, charged by prayer or meditation.

The Unity Principle is the premise behind this. Negative land imprints have negative consciousness. When you place a prayer stone with positive consciousness within the area, or the circle of a negative land imprint, the two will look to balance each other out. This will increase the consciousness of the circle and raise the net reading of the area. If the prayer stone has a vortex, it will generally be much stronger than the negative space unless it contains a negative energy vortex.

How much influence a talisman will have on a space will be dependent upon a variety of factors, such as the relative strength of the talisman and the negative land imprint compared to each other and how much each is fed with the underlying intention that created it after the placement. For example, reinforcing the talisman with periodic praying or doing ceremony when you go there will help. You can also replace the talisman and bring the old one back to your home to be replenished in the same fashion it was created.

Exhibit 10-1 shows how a talisman with a vortex attached to it can restore the flow of prana. On the left the flow of prana is disturbed as seen by the tilted arrows. On the right, much of the prana has returned to its normal flow (straight ahead) as seen with the horizontal arrows. Notice how the area of normalization in the flow of prana is confined to the area of the samskara's whirlpool.

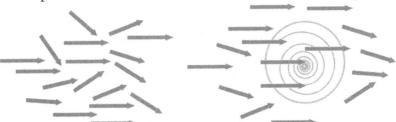

Exhibit 10-1. Talisman restores the flow of prana.

Using prayer stones is similar to the Native American custom of countering a violent or negative action with a positive one. For example, if they killed a deer they would counter the action by giving thanks or a blessing to the deer. Black Elk, a Lakota Medicine Man, known for his visions and wisdom, tells how he would honor the willows that he was going to cut down for his sweat lodge.[5]

You can use prayer stones to raise the consciousness of any space from your work site to your local park. Anyone who has read the *Autobiography of a Yogi*, by Paramhansa Yogananda,[6] will remember how he constantly said that the spiritual vibrations of a place could protect or uplift someone, and how he regrettably lost his beloved Kashi when the student was removed from the school (high vibrations) at a particularly vulnerable time in his life.

Kashi was one of Yogananda's most beloved and brilliant students. The Yogi had been foretold that Kashi would die at a young age so he went out of his way to protect the youth. One summer the Yogi went away on a trip and told the young Kashi not to leave the ashram for any purpose realizing that the *spiritual vibrations* there would protect the youth. Unfortunately, Kashi's father came to the ashram and for fifteen days badgered the boy to come home for a few days and visit his mother in Calcutta. At his home Kashi ate contaminated food and ended up contracting and dying of cholera.

An enhanced field improves the chances for more co-creations with Mother Earth and opens up new vistas and aspects of Mother Earth as you begin to sense and experience things that have been blocked by negative thoughts. Living in a positive environment is critical to our well-being and spiritual development. A home with a weak or compromised field will have detrimental effects.

What makes talismans an attractive tool is you can leave them at a space to work 24/7 so you don't have to be there all the time. They are great for public spaces where you may not be able to meditate or smudge. A small stone, remember they can be tiny, can be left in a public space and not draw any attention. Sometimes I dig a little hole and embed them in the ground, I don't cover them, but covering them would be okay as long as they are made of Cosmic Prana. I often leave them in places where violent acts have occurred. They can also be left at places that are particularly pernicious, reducing the need for you to be there.

Personally I view clearing space the same way as taking medicine over a period of time. I am not an advocate of going some place only one time for a cleansing and being done. Instead I see healing a space as a series of steps or stages. Sometimes you can clear something immediately, but it usually takes a few visits or more.

I constantly create prayer stones by placing them in bags next to me when I meditate. I also charge them by using them to make circles or other structures. As long as they are in the circle of my draw they will be picking up my intention. They are a great tool.

Protection, Blocking Detrimental Energies

Talismans can be used to protect oneself against detrimental energies such as EMF's. The positive samskara of the talisman will attempt to balance out with the samskaras it comes in contact with. This may not totally block out detrimental energies, but can usually diminish their impact.

I usually keep a talisman, a meditation cushion, in front of my computer screen to reduce the emission of detrimental energies. The amount of reduction will be influenced by the size of the computer screen and the strength of the talisman. A strong talisman may reduce the field of emanations projected from a smaller computer screen; for example if it projects detrimental energies out 4 feet the talisman may cut it down to 2 feet. For a larger computer screen it may have less of an impact and only reduce the amount of emanations you come in contact with. It may have a minimal affect on very large computer screens requiring you to use several talismans.

Exhibit 10-2 shows how a prayer stone placed in front of you while using a computer can protect you by reducing the amount of detrimental energies that reach you. Notice how the talisman creates

If the vortex does not appear to be spot specific you should try to determine if it formed in the center of a larger area where spiritual activity took place. Scour the surrounding area for stone mounds, large stones, stone circles or aspects of Mother Earth. If you find something, assume it is the far fringe of the spiritual area; this is a gross assumption that is far from perfect. Take a rough measurement of the distance (walking is fine) from the aspect to the vortex to discover the radius of the sacred area.

Continue walking in the same direction, away from the vortex, the same distance as the radius. Next walk around the periphery of the vortex at the distance you just recorded in a circular pattern. If you find any other stones or aspects of Mother Earth it will give you more confirmation. This is not an exact method and will require trial and error, but once you have some experience, and put some time in at a site, you may well be amazed at what you find. Remember it takes time to begin to know and feel a space and this can help speed up the effort.

Again you are making gross assumptions; still this is a useful tool.

Reinvigorate

A particular space, stone formation or talisman needs to be periodically reinvigorated. This is especially true if you are working with a negative space. The transformation of consciousness is a dynamic process as it is constantly interacting with what it comes in contact with. Land imprints and talismans can be degraded through direct contact, by being in close proximity to a ley line carrying negative consciousness, or from being bombarded by technological electro-pollution.

Similarly sacred places need to be continually reinvigorated with prayer, ritual and positive intentions and actions. Unfortunately people that visit can come with selfish purposes or are gawkers who see the sacred site as a physical space rather than a place of transformation and spiritual growth. Whenever you visit sacred space make sure to honor it and come with the purest of intentions.

Stay dedicated and vigilant in your effort to heal and help Mother Earth and she will shower you with her blessings!

Chapter 11

A Transformative Force

We have an incredibly dynamic and loving relationship with Mother Earth. Our good, or bad intentions have a profound impact upon Her. Our environmental crisis is a crisis of our hearts. Our hate, our anger, our violence, and our selfishness ravage Her. The carbon-producing activities we credit for depleting the ozone level, and the technology that creates electro-pollution and geopathic stress, are symptomatic of the larger problem in our hearts. They are technologies we have developed based upon exploitation rather than cooperation; they are destructive technologies that employ explosion and heat as Viktor Schauberger taught. They reflect our exploitive and destructive intention. The world needs love.

We are linked to each other in profound ways. We are constantly in contact with the consciousness of others through the geographic samskaras we walk through each day. The many circles in our lives connect us to others. What you do matters to others and what others do matters to you. We are one. We cannot escape this with a cabin in the woods or a spiritual path of isolation. Because we are collectively bound to each other, we must work together to create a better world so that we may all advance.

Work with Mother Earth

I hope you use the knowledge I have shared with you about vortices. Vortices are a wonderful tool for healing Mother Earth and all of life. They can hasten your spiritual development and be used to study sacred sites. Vortices are also a tool to see what is going on beyond what our eyes can discern in our world.

Finding a vortex is a great joy. I started this book talking about a wonderful spiritual experience I had within a vortex I found on a mountaintop in Vermont. There are similar vortices all over the world in deserts, by the water, deep in woods, in cities and in all sorts of places. These are places close to your home you can find with a little effort, places where you can transcend time and absorb the mother's milk of consciousness of those who created it.

Not only is there a benefit to praying or meditating in a vortex, there is also a great joy of accomplishment and connection to Mother Earth that comes with finding one. In 2010 I got a call from a gentleman in Arizona who had read my article on vortices in the American Society of Dowsers 50th anniversary issue of their Digest (magazine) and wanted to thank me. He was elated because he had found a vortex at the end of his bed where he did healings. Prior to reading my article he knew nothing about the formation process of a vortex or even the notion of looking for one.

Become a Keeper

Native Americans have a wonderful custom of creating sacred space. When they would travel they periodically stopped to do ceremony, pray and give thanks. They would make pilgrimages to special aspects of Mother Earth, or go into the woods to pray and fast in the hopes of receiving a vision. Many of the vortices and vortex rings I find by waterfalls, on mountaintops, deep in the woods, or where there must have clearly been an intersection of Native trails, were blessed by the intentions and prayers of Native Americans. Thank you.

I ask that you please consider taking this practice to heart. I spend much of my time purifying sacred sites and making space sacred. During these times I have gained and learned so much.

Jesus said, "Give and you shall receive."[1] The bounty I have received has been enormous, a hastening of my spiritual development, achieving higher meditative states, a feeling of well-being, insights, and an understanding of Mother Earth. Apply the principles I have taught you about vortices to purify and make space sacred so that others may some day benefit from your blessing. In doing this you will develop a better connection to and understanding of Mother Earth. Pick a space to clear, leave a talisman, stop on a journey to pray, make a welcome circle on a trail. Pass it on.

Once you have committed to creating sacred space you may wish to step it up and become a Keeper. A Keeper is one who maintains and oversees a particular sacred site or feature within it. This is an ancient practice that has been lost and needs to be revived. The word Keeper is my terminology, but the premise is ancient.

On several occasions I have had visions or heard voices where Keepers once practiced their art. One such time, I was on South Hill at the southern end of Canandaigua Lake, in the Finger Lakes Region of New York. While meditating on one of the larger stone mounds, I heard a stern and mildly prideful voice within say, "Four Keepers took care of this mound." The implication was that it was a succession of four Keepers over a period of years who maintained, watched over and guided visiting pilgrims. Because of this experience I now call this *The Keepers' Area.*

I am a Keeper for several sites. Over time, as your relationship with the space grows, you will be tapping into the collective samskara of the space. For me this has been connecting with the spirit of a group I call Spirit Keepers who maintained the Fields of Consciousness in the holiest of holy places in Mother Earth's soul. From their lingering samskaras and spirits I learned so much about working with stone and practices such as the "empty circle technique" I have shared with you.

Learn to Dowse

If you are not a dowser at this time, I strongly encourage you to learn dowsing. Dowsing will allow you to find vortices and help you to gauge geographic samskaras as well as improve your connection to Mother Earth.

As noted earlier there are host of not-for-profit dowsing organizations around the world, such as the American Society of Dowsers and British Society of Dowsers (see the listing in the appendix.) Most have numerous local chapters that will teach you to dowse for free, or at a very nominal cost. The national organizations hold conferences and workshops where you can not only improve your dowsing skills, but also learn about Mother Earth, healing, and the unseen world.

When you gather with experienced dowsers, you will gain from their knowledge as you merge with their circles. They can help improve your dowsing skills and show you aspects of Mother Earth. Some may even be able to point out an energy vortex to you.

Develop a Strong Bond with Mother Earth

A strong bond with Mother Earth is critical if you want to work with vortices. Whether you wish to create a vortex or find one, your success is incumbent upon your relationship with Mother Earth. Many healers can feel and find a vortex of Earth Prana; but to find a vortex of Cosmic Prana or higher aspects of Mother Earth, you need to have a strong bond with Her.

She is your Mother, she nourishes you and can teach you. Having a strong relationship with Her can significantly improve your health and well-being. This relationship will also increase your ability to co-create a vortex with Her.

Ideally, you should try to gain sentience of Mother Earth. To be able to sense Her is to know Her. Having sentience of Mother Earth will improve your interaction with Her. This will help you pick up on the atmosphere or vibe of where you are for both the good and for the bad. Over time it will also help you be able to distinguish between energy and consciousness; energy feeds the energy body and is needed for health, while consciousness feeds the soul.

Spiritual exercises, prayer and mediation, done within special aspects of Mother Earth, will broaden your relationship with Her. Find such a place close to your home and visit as often as you can.

Look Upon Nature

Spend some time by the bank of a stream or by a small waterfall. Watch and observe the whirlpools form and dissipate. They are like the circles in your life coming and going, some staying. Watch the larger influences. See how a twig moves. Observe how life responds to the movement of water. See the patterns of your life and the greater world manifesting its forms in the movement of water and creation of vortices in front of you. Isn't Mother Earth wonderful?

A vortex is a magical thing, a blessing from Mother Earth and God. In a world that has been layered over for centuries with the consciousness of negativity, violence, and technology, a vortex has the ability to heal and protect you. It can also heal Mother Earth and negate the many wounds and scars we have afflicted upon Her. A vortex has the power to reverse the most hideous damage and restore and rejuvenate. It has the power to transform.

Approach Mother Earth with the best of intentions, the purest of heart, and with the biggest of dreams, and she will eventually come to you and work with you. A vortex is only one step in a long and beautiful journey.

Love, give, heal, do unto others, practice ahimsa, pray, meditate and Mother Earth may bless you with a vortex.

Notes

Chapter 2 Consciousness Manifesting

1. Sri Aurobindo. *Letters on Yoga*. Volume 22, Section Five, Planes and Parts of The Being, 236.

2. Adi Shankara. *Vivekachudamani of Shri Shankaracharya*, Translation by Swami Madhavananda, Advaita Ashrama: Calcutta, India Sixth Edition, 1957 #391.

3. Adi Shankara. *Crest Jewel of Discrimination* (Viveka-Chudamani.) Translated by Swami Prabhavananda and Christopher Isherwood, Vedanta Press, Hollywood California, 53, 64, 68, 70.

4. Saraswati, Satyasangananda. *Sri Vijnana Bhairava Tantra: The Ascent*. Yoga Publications Trust/Bihar School of Yoga, December 2003, 23.

5. Samkhya.

6. Patanjali. *Four chapters on Freedom, Commentary on the Yoga Sutras of Patanjali*. Swami Satyananda Saraswati, translator. Yoga Publications Trust: Munger, Bihar, India, 2002, 2:21.

7. This is a very broad definition.

8. Bhagavad-Gita 13:20.

9. Vritti's have a strong consciousness component, but are not pure consciousness. This is because our focus and thinking is on the Physical Plane. The spiral form of our thoughts, vritti's is not unique to our thinking. Rather, the spiral form is a reflection of consciousness as it descends into the material. In other words the spiral shape is the form and movement consciousness has in the lower planes.

10. Geoff Ward. *Spirals the patterns of Existence*. Green Magic: England, 2006, 1.

11. Theodor Schwenk. *Sensitive Chaos, The Creation of Flowing Forms in Water and Air*. Rudolf Steiner Press: London, 1965, 24.

12. Michael S. Schneider. *A Beginner's Guide to Constructing the Universe, The Mathematical Archetypes of Nature, Art, and Science*. HarperCollins: New York, 1995, 139.

13. *Three Initiates* (believed to be William Walker Atkinson and possibly others.) *The Kybalion, A Study of the Hermetic Philosophy of Ancient Egypt and Greece*. Rough Draft Publishing: 2012.

Chapter 3 Vortices That Attach

1. Bhagavad-Gita: 2:62-63.

2. Meher Baba. *Discourses*. Shaeriar Press: Myrtle Beach, South Carolina, 1995, 10.

3. William Wordsworth. "Lines composed a few miles above Tintern Abbey in revisiting the bank of Wye during a tour. July 13, 1798." *Norton Anthology of Poetry*, W.W. Norton: New York, 1970, 557.

4. T. C. Lethbridge. *The Essential T. Lethbridge*, Edited by Tom Graves and Janet Hoult. Granada Publishing: London England, 1980, 38.

5. William Tiller, Walter Dibble, and Michael Kohane. *Conscious Acts of Creation*. Pavior Publishing: 2001, 5.

6. Robins, L. N., Helzer, J. E., Hesselbrock, M. and Wish, E. (2010), "Vietnam Veterans Three Years after Vietnam: How Our Study Changed Our View of Heroin." The American Journal on Addictions, 19: 203–211. doi: 10.1111/j.1521-0391.2010.00046.x. Originally published in *Problems of Drug Dependence, 1977, Proceedings of the Thirty-Ninth Annual Scientific Meeting of the Committee on Problems*

of Drug Dependence. Online at: http://onlinelibrary.wiley.com/doi/10.1111/j.1521-0391.2010.00046.x/abstract.

7. Alix Spiegel. 'What Vietnam Taught Us About Breaking Bad Habits.' NPR: January 2, 2012, http://www.npr.org/blogs/health/2012/01/02/144431794/what-vietnam-taught-us-about-breaking-bad-habits.

8. C. G. Jung. "Man and Earth", *Collected Works Volume 10, Civilization in Transition, Volume 10;* Bollingen Series. Princeton University Press: 1968, c1958, 49.

9. Claire Sylvia with William Novak. *A Change of Heart, A Memoir.* Little, Brown and Company: New York, 1997, 84, 104, 107. 184-187.

10. Ibid., 137-142.

11. Masaru Emoto. *The Hidden Message in Water.* Atria Books: New York, 2001, 45-97.

12. Bahá'í: "Blessed is he who preferreth his brother before himself."Baha'u'llah, Tablets of Baha'u'llah, 71.

Buddhism:"Hurt not others in ways that you yourself would find hurtful." Udana-Varga, 5:18.

Christianity:"All things whatsoever ye would that men should do to you, do ye even so to them." Matthew 7:12.

Confucianism: "Do not unto others what you would not have them do unto you." Analects 15:23.

Hinduism:"This is the sum of duty: do naught unto others which would cause you pain if done to you." Mahabharata 5:1517.

Islam:"No one of you is a believer until he desires for his brother that which he desires for himself."- Sunnah.

Jainism: "In happiness and suffering, in joy and grief, we should regard all creatures as we regard our own self."- Lord Mahavira, 24th Tirthankara.

Judaism: "What is hateful to you, do not to your fellow man. That is the law: all the rest is commentary." Talmud, Shabbat 31a

Native American:"Respect for all life is the foundation." The Great Law of Peace.

Sikhism:"Don't create enmity with anyone as God is within everyone." Guru Arjan Devji 259, Guru Granth Sahib.

Zoroastrianism: "That nature only is good when it shall not do unto another whatever is not good for its own self."Dadistan-i-Dinik, 94:5.

13. Geoff Ward. *Spirals the Patterns of Existence*. Green Magic: England 2006, 30.

14. Viktor Schauberger. *Living Water, Viktor Schauberger and the Secrets of Natural Energy*, by Olof Alexandersson. Translated by Kit and Charles Zweigbergk. Gateway Publishing: Dublin Ireland, 1990, 77.

15. The timeless wisdom is to look within not out. "As a boat on the water is swept away by a strong wind, even one of the senses on which the mind focuses can carry away a man's intelligence." (Bhagavad-Gita 2.67) "The embodied soul may be restricted from sense enjoyment, though the taste for sense objects remains. But, ceasing such engagements by experiencing a higher taste, he is fixed in consciousness." (Bhagavad-Gita 2:59)

16. Viktor Schauberger, *Living Water, Viktor Schauberger and the Secrets of Natural Energy*, by Olof Alexandersson, Translated by Kit and Charles Zweigbergk, Gateway Publishing, Dublin Ireland, 1990, 77, 78.

17. Theodor Schwenk. *Sensitive Chaos, The Creation of Flowing Forms in Water and Air*. Rudolf Steiner Press: London, 1965, 39.

18. T. C. Lethbridge. *Ghost and Divining Rod*. Routledge & Kegan Paul: London, 1963.

Chapter 4 Our Bond With Mother Earth

1. Spirituality & The Brain (God Helmet, Shiva/Shakti Helmet): http://www.shaktitechnology.com.

Michael A. Persinger and Gyslaine F. Lafrenière. *Space-time transients and unusual events.* Burnham Inc. Pub, 1977.

Winifred Gallagher. *The Power of Place, How Our Surroundings Shape Out Thoughts, Emotions and Actions.* Harper Perennial: New York, 1993, 89-98.

Barbara Bradley Hagerty. *Fingerprints of God, The Search for the Science of Spirituality.* Riverhead Books: New York, 2009, 134-142.

2. Susan Blackmore, writer and skeptical investigator of the paranormal said she had one of the more extraordinary experiences of her life at Persinger's lab. Dr. Michael Shermer, Founding Publisher of *Skeptic* magazine, Executive Director of the Skeptics Society, and columnist for *Scientific American* reported that he felt a 'sensed presence' and had an out-of-body experience. Atheist and focal critique of religious belief, Richard Dawkins, experienced a range of somatic sensations but nothing else. http://www.innerworlds.50megs.com/The_God_Helmet_Debate.htm.

3. By reducing mystical experiences to neural activity in the brain, the God Helmet has raised a lot of concern and debate in religious circles. In her book *Fingerprints of God: What Science Is Learning About the Brain and Spiritual Experience* Barbara Hagerty notes this was one of Persinger's goals. The God Helmet substantiates much of what I have learned about ultimate reality and in doing so reaffirms my belief in God even more.

4. Swami Niranjanananda Saraswati. *Prana Pranayama, Prana Vidya.* Bihar School of Yoga: Munger, Bihar, 1998, 4.

5. Richard Gerber. *Vibrational Medicine.* Bear & Co: 2001, 475.

Chapter 5 The Birth of an Energy Vortex

1. Starhawk. *Spiral Dance, A Rebirth of the Ancient Religion of the Goddess.* Harper San Francisco: San Francisco, California, 1999, 36.

2.   http://geomancy.org/e-zine/1996/winter/gathering-earth-energies/index.html.

3. Guy Underwood. *Pattern of the Past*. Abelard & Shuman LTD: New York, 1973, 39.

4. Alanna Moore. *Divining Earth Spirit*. Python Press: 2nd Edition, 2004, 21.

5. J. Krappraff. "The Spiral in Nature, Myth and Mathematics," in *Spiral Symmetry*, edited by Istvan Hargittai and Clifford A. Pickover, World Scientific: New Jersey, 1992, 15-16.

6. Theodor Schwenk,. *Sensitive Chaos, The Creation of Flowing Forms in Water and Air*. Rudolf Steiner Press: London, 1965, 44.

Chapter 6 Bathed in Bliss and Well Being

1. Janet Macrae. *Therapeutic touch A practical Guide*. Alfred A. Knopf: 1996; 4, 17.

2. Robert Gerber. *Vibrational Medicine*. 2000, 529.

3. Andrew Newberg and Mark Robert Waldman. *How God Changes Your Brain-Breakthrough Findings from a Leading Neuroscientist*, Ballantine Books, New York 2009, pages 6-7.

4. Adi Shankara. *Vivekachudamani of Shri Shankaracharya*, Translation by Swami Madhavananda,. Advaita Ashrama: Calcutta, India, Sixth Edition, 1957 #361.

5. Violence, selfish acts, greed and a focus on money and wealth may in fact diminish your inflow of prana.

6. Patanjali. *Four chapters on Freedom, Commentary on the Yoga Sutras of Patanjali*, by Swami Satyananda Saraswati. Yoga Publications Trust: Munger, Bihar, India, 2202, Sutra 2;25, 178.

7. Ibid.

Chapter 7 Negative Vortices

1. Isaiah 24:1.

2. Isaiah 24:5.

3. Ezekiel 5:6-17.

4. Jeremiah 14:1.

5. Amos 9:4-9.

6. Lawrence and Phoebe Bendit. *The Etheric body of Man*. Quest Books, Wheaton, Illinois, 1989, 26-27.

7. A. P. Dubrov. *The Geomagnetic Field and Life, Geomagneticbiology*. Plenum Press: New York, 1978.

8. Dr. Robert Gerber. *Vibrational Medicine*. Bear & Co: Santa Fe, NM, 463.

9. Ibid.

10. Clinton Ober, Stephen Sinatra (M.D.) and Martin Zucker. *Earthing, The Most Important Health Discovery Ever?*. Basic Health Publications: Laguna Beach, California, 2010, 13.

11. David Cowan and Chris Arnold. *Ley Lines and Earth Energies*. Adventures Unlimited Press: Kempton, Illinois, 2003, 133-135.

12. http://www.professional-house-clearing.com/von-pohl.html .

Chapter 8 Creating Vortices

1. To learn more about Bill Attride read his blog: http://astrologerbillattride.typepad.com/astrologer-bill-attride/#tp.

2. Krishnamurti Foundation of America, http://www.kfa.org/.

3. See *The Way Home, Making Heaven on Earth*, by Madis Senner for a more detailed discussion of why technology and science are destructive.

4. Becker, Dr. Robert. *Cross Currents: the Promise of Electromedicine, the Perils of Electropollution*. Tarcher: Los Angeles, California, 1990, 187.

5. Ibid. 146.

6. Fields of consciousness emanate consciousness; divine aspects of love, compassion, service, self-sacrifice... Gaia's Soul, Fields of Consciousness, http://www.jubileeinitiative.org/gaiassoul.html.

7. Mother Earth's soul is in the greater upstate NY area that extends into other states in the northeast and to the west and to the south.

8. Elizabeth Cady Stanton, Susan B. Anthony, Fredrick Douglass, Harriet Tubman, Charles Gandison Finney among others. See Gaia's Soul--Birthplace of the spiritual, the prophetic and justice' http://www.jubileeinitiative.org/gaiassoul5.html.

9. Spirit Keepers are the people that maintained and watched over the holiest of holy places in Mother Earth's soul in central NY. I have learned much from them. To learn more go to: http://www.jubileeinitiative.org/spiritkeepers.html

10. Mircea Eliade. *Patterns in Comparative Religion.* Sheed & Ward: New York,1958, 370.

11. Ibid. 371.

Chapter 9 The Mystical Form

1. Jill Purce. *The Mystic Spiral, Journey of the Soul.* Avon: New York, 1974, Number 59.

2. Starhawk. *Spiral Dance, A Rebirth of the Ancient Religion of the Goddess.* Harper San Francisco. San Francisco California, 1999, 258-259.

3. Francis Hitching. *Earth Magic.* Pocket Books: 1978., 252.

4. Ibid. 253.

5. By doing samyama, an intense contemplation that involves dhyana, dharana and Samadhi at the same time.

6. Sutra 3:21.

7. Sutra 3:25.

8. As I noted earlier the Iranian mystic Meher Baba said that samskaras formed an enclosure that blocksour perspective, so it is with comprehending the awesome beauty and power of the spiral.

9. Mircea Eliade. *Patterns in Comparative Religion*. Sheed & Ward: New York, 1958, page 189.

10. Viktor Schauberger. *Living Water, Viktor Schauberger and the Secrets of Natural Energy*, by Olof Alexandersson, Translated by Kit and Charles Zweigbergk. Gateway Publishing: Dublin Ireland, 1990, 145.

11. Steve Herbert, water dowser and instructor, in an email to me February 27, 2013.

12.C. G. Jung. *The Collected Works*, Vol. V. Princeton, NJ : Bollingen Foundation. Princeton University Press: 1967, Volume 12, #325

13. Phi, or the golden ratio is based upon the Fibonacci sequence where the amount of increase in a sequence of numbers is the sum of the previous two numbers, 21, 34, and 55(21+34). 89 (55+34), When we apply this sequence in a ratio (a +b)/a= a/b = 55/34 = 89/55 = 1.618 = phi.

14. The Fibonacci sequence is the sum of the previous two numbers and begins with 0 and 1; 0, 1, 1, 2, 3, 5, 8, 13, 21, 34, 55, 89, 144...

15. Ralph Nelson Elliot. *Nature's Law, The Secret of the Universe*. SN Publishing: 2010, 27.

16. Robert R. Prechter, Jr.. *The Wave Principle of Human Social Behavior and the New Science of Socionomics*. New Classics Library: Gainesville, Georgia, 2002.

17. Matthew Cross and Robert Friedman. *The Divine Code of Da Vinci, Fibonacci, Einstein and You*. Hoshin Media: Stamford, Connecticut, 2009.

18. For a review of the Foundation of Light go to: http://www.jubileeinitiative.org/sacredfol.html.

19. "Do Labyrinths Have a Design Flaw?"
http://www.jubileeinitiative.org/labyrinths.html.
20. Dr Karl S. Kruszelnicki, "Black hole science key to WiFi"
http://www.abc.net.au/science/articles/2012/09/18/3590519.htm
#.UcCY7diurAw.
21. Iroquois.

Chapter 10 Simple Things That You Can Do

1. Clinton Ober, Stephen Sinatra, (M.D.) and Martin Zucker. *Earthing, The Most Important Health Discovery Ever?* Basic Health Publications: Laguna Beach, California, 2010.
2. See Duke Johnson, MD, *The Optimal Health Revolution*, Benbella Books, Dallas, Texas, 2008; Nancy Appleton, Ph.D, *Stopping Inflammation, Relieving the Cause of Degenerative Disease*, SquareOne Publishers, Garden City Park, NY, 2005. There are many more.
3. Ober, Clinton& Sinatra, Stephen (M.D.) & Zucker, Martin; *Earthing, The Most Important Health Discovery Ever?*, Basic Health Publications: Laguna Beach, California, 2010 15.
4. Ibid. 76-81.
5. Black Elk; *The Sacred Pipe, Black Elk's Account of the Seven Rites of the Oglala Sioux*, Recorded and Edited by Joseph Epes Brown. University of Oklahoma Press: Norman, Oklahoma, 1953, 48.
6. Paramahansa Yogananda. *Autobiography of a Yogi*. Crystal Clarity Publishers: Nevada City, CA , 1946c, 2005.

Chapter 11 A Transformative Force

1. Luke 6:38.

Appendix

1. The Haudenosaunee prophet the Peacemaker planted the Tree of Peace on the shores of Onondaga lake and gave us the Great Law of Peace upon which the principles of American democracy is based upon.

2. See The Peacmaker's Sanctuary

http://www.jubileeinitiative.org/sacredpeacemaker.html.

Appendix

Connecting with Mother Earth
Dowsing Organizations
Sites on Mother Earth
Visit Mother Earth's Soul
Mother Earth Press

Connecting with Mother Earth

Like any relationship, your connection to Mother Earth will depend upon your commitment to and focus on Her. You need to commit to Her and those who honor Her, and eliminate the circles in your life that harm or are opposed to Her, such as technology or groups that trample or are dismissive of Mother Earth. For most this means wholesale radical change. Would you belong to a hate or racist group if you embraced equality, or had friends who were targeted by such a group? Of course not. So if you want to embrace Mother Earth, you need to similarly eliminate technology and other circles that are dedicated to Her destruction.

You need to make your connection to Mother Earth a quest you build upon and one that remains a lifelong journey. There is no ten-point plan, but rather a program you develop yourself. Look within and ask yourself how you can develop a relationship with Mother Earth.

Reflect, contemplate on how you can better get to know Mother Earth. Explore. Embrace the customs of those who do have a strong bond with Her; be like a Native American and give thanks to Her, or perform ceremony in Her honor. Go to a meeting of environmentalists; attend a Solstice celebration, or a pagan gathering. You don't have to commit to any of these, just explore and learn in order to see what fits you.

You are looking to change your focus away from our modern day society's destructive and parasitic relationship with Mother Earth, to one that is symbiotic and based upon love. Try to see Her in the world around you in the sky, the sea, the mountains and not the accoutrements of modern society, such as malls, fast food restaurants, concrete and telephone poles. For example, when you gaze out see the trees and not the building behind them.

There are a host of authors you should consider reading for inspiration and direction. Here are a few. There are many more; explore, investigate search:

Father Thomas Berry, was a Catholic priest and a strong advocate of eco-spirituality and deep ecology.

Black Elk, Waká (Medicine Man and Holy Man) of the Oglala Lakota (Sioux)

Bill McKibben, a well-known environmental activist.

Starhawk, activist and pagan who helped launch the neo-pagan movement.

Michael J. Cohen, a professor who is sentient of Mother Earth and has a good book out titled *Re-connecting with Nature*.

Consider taking up hobbies such as gardening or hiking that involve Mother Earth.

Try to gain sentience of Her; to sense and feel Her is to know Her. Begin by trying to be able to sense energy and then move onto consciousness. To experience energy go to an energy healer or become one yourself. Learn to dowse for energy lines or Earth Chakras with a group of dowers.

Remember you are on a quest wandering like Buddha did to find Enlightenment, only you are looking to build a strong samskara or circle with Mother Earth.

Dowsing Organizations

There are many dowsing organizations that offer classes. Here is a listing of some of the national dowsing organizations:

American Society of Dowsers: http://www.dowsers.org.

British Society of Dowsers: http://www.britishdowsers.org.

Canadian Society of Dowsers: http://www.canadiandowsers.org.

Canadian Society of Questers: http://www.questers.ca.

Dowsers of NSW: http://www.dowsingaustralia.com.

Dowsing Society of Victoria: http://www.dsv.org.au/index.shtml.

Irish Society of Diviners: http://www.irishdiviners.com.

New Zealand Society of Dowsing and Radionics Inc.: http://www.dowsingnewzealand.org.nz/index.html.

Books, Private Organizations:

If you are looking for dowsing books, the ASD (American Society of Dowsers) has a comprehensive listing, as do several other dowsing organizations; by purchasing from them you will be supporting them.

Joe Smith was a Trustee of ASD who has passed. He and his wife, Martha, were active members who tirelessly served the dowsing community. He was known for his dancing pendulums and numerous stories that can be accessed at: http://www.susantom.com/joestories.html . There is a DVD you can buy of Joe and his wife teaching dowsing at: http://www.in2it.ca/videos.htm.

Nigel Percy and his wife, Maggie, have a wonderful website to teach you how to dowse, Discovering Dowsing. I am on a listserve with Nigel and have always found him to be incredibly knowledgeable and helpful to others, especially those just starting to learn how to dowse.

www.http://discoveringdowsing.com/.

Sig Lonegren got his Masters Degree in dowsing. He is a fount of knowledge, particularly on Earth energies and sacred sites. He has been very helpful to many including myself. He has an excellent book out on dowsing, *Spiritual Dowsing*. He has written one of the definitive book on pendulums, *The Pendulum Kit*.

Tom Graves is a well-respected dowser who has written several books such as *The Diviner's Handbook: A Guide to the Timeless Art of Dowsing*.

Toronto Dowsers (private organization): For those living in the Toronto, Ontario Canada area, Marilyn Gang offers a very interesting series of classes and speakers.

http://www.dowsers.info/toronto/toronto.htm.

Other Sources on Mother Earth

Mother Earth Prayers—Information about Mother Earth, her cosmology and sacred sites in upstate New York in the heart of Mother Earth's soul: www.motherearthprayers.org.

Geomantica Magazine—Australian Dowser, Alanna Moore, has a free and informative online magazine about Mother Earth, detrimental energy, dowsing and more. I encourage everyone interested in Mother Earth and the harm that we are doing her to register to receive info at http://www.geomantica.com/.

Mid Atlantic Geomancy--http://geomancy.org/ Sig Lonegren has an excellent archive of old articles on Earth energies/mysteries, sacred sites and more.

Earth Energies Group British Society of Dowsers, http://www.britishdowsers.org/EEG_site/home.shtml.

The Geomancy Group: A group page for geomancers in the UK; http://www.geomancygroup.org/index.html.

Tree Whisperer Western New York. Clarisa is blessed to be sentient of Mother Earth http://www.treewhispererwny.com.

Visit Mother Earth's Soul

In the summer of 2002 God asked me to get people to pray around Onondaga Lake in Syracuse, New York. This began my quest to learn more about and connect with Mother Earth. I soon realized the greater area of upstate New York has been a very transformative force in shaping our collective global consciousness for the better. I learned about a special aspect of Mother Earth behind this transformation that I call Fields of Consciousness: the birthplace of ley lines.

I encourage you to visit Mother Earth's soul. My Mother Earth Prayers website (www.motherearthprayers.org) has a listing of sacred sites (http://www.jubileeinitiative.org/sacredsites.html) you can visit. Each site listed contains a description of the Fields of Consciousness found there, as well other aspects of Mother Earth. By praying, doing ritual, or meditating at them you will help fortify them. In other words, your good intentions will make them stronger, which will increase the potency of the consciousness emanating from them thereby giving the ley lines a more potent charge before they begin traversing the world. The belief is this increased dosage will help nourish our individual and collective consciousness and make a better world.

I have witnessed first hand the transformative power of prayer done at Fields of Consciousness. In the fall of 2000 when I returned to Syracuse I was very upset by the level of violence and killings in the city. I prayed to God to guide me to help bring about peace. In the fall of 2002 God answered my prayers and instructed me to organize a prayer vigil at a specific location on the shores of Onondaga Lake[1] in Syracuse, NY. At the time I did not know anything about Fields of Consciousness or that the location, which we subsequently named the Peacemaker's Sanctuary, was situated on such a field. We held a prayer vigil the Friday after Thanksgiving at the Peacemaker's Sanctuary[2] in 2002 and I went and prayed there every day until January 19, 2003 when the city had its first homicide. That was one of the longest recent periods without a homicide in Syracuse and it marked the peak in homicides.

A visit to Mother Earth's Soul will also help nourish your soul and better help you feel consciousness. It can be a very transformative experience.

Please visit.

Mother Earth Press

For more information on other books and products go to: www.motherearthpress.net.

Glossary

Amulet—an object charged by focused concentration often for a specific purpose. The amulet picks up and retains the creator's intention; basically a samskara (thought) attaches to the object, which charges it. Amulets are traditionally created for protection.

Chakra—is a spinning wheel, or vortex that facilitates the movement of prana in the human subtle body and Mother Earth. It consists of a vortex, which pulls in prana released by a duct at a distance, and two nadis (energy lines) below the vortex that are at 90° to each other in the shape of a right angle which transport the prana. Chakras are often clumped together in a series, creating a larger structure, or chakra. A chakra is a permanent structure and unlike an energy vortex is not created through human intention.

Chi—see prana.

Circles—are the various relationships in your life, both conscious and unconscious. A circle is a vortex that looks to unite and merge the various elements within it.

Consciousness—is what you are focused on or paying attention to; it has morality to it running along the continuum from the divine to the demonic.

Consciousness component—is the consciousness and energy makeup, or spirit and matter makeup of something. Ultimately it is about how much consciousness something has, with higher consciousness having a more spiritual or divine aspect.

Consciousness, negative—is closer to the law of self-interest, violence and materiality.

Consciousness, positive—is closer to the golden rule and the law of love.

Consciousness, pure—is indescribable; it is the divine.

Consciousness quotient—is a rough measure of our spiritual growth. It is that part of your being that is here to be transformed.

Consciousness reading—is the measure of a geographic samskara's or object's consciousness and measures whether the underlying consciousness is more positive/divine or negative/demonic-like.

Cosmic Prana—is prana with a high consciousness component. It is the prana that we attract during meditation and from selfless and loving acts. It nourishes our soul.

Dark night of the soul—refers to the purification of our being. It is the latter stages of our spiritual evolution when we have to face our deficiencies such as our anxieties, angers, fears, jealousies and temptations before they are purged. It is an acceleration of the burning off of our samskaras as we spiritually evolve. After we travel through the dark night of our soul, we achieve a higher state of consciousness that has been called many things by different faith traditions, such as Enlightenment, Samadhi, Ecstasy, Super Consciousness....

Draw—how much energy, or prana, we attract during a particular activity such as meditating or healing. A barometer of our capability at performing the activity-- the more draw the better.

Duct—circular in shape, helps with the movement of prana. It radiates prana in all directions, or 360°, which is then pulled toward a chakra in the distance.

Earth Chakra—is a chakra that facilitates the movement of Earth Prana.

Earth Prana—is a coarse prana with a low consciousness component and the only prana that circulates in both the atmosphere and in the Earth.

Electro-pollution—the disruption to Mother Earth and the human subtle body by emanations and the underlying consciousness of electrical devices, digital technology and other man-made gizmos.

Empty circle technique—is a method to create an energy vortex by making a circle where you wish a vortex to form and then meditating or praying around its radius.

Energy body—is that particular human subtle body connected to the Energy Plane.

Energy line—is a line that transports prana, or energy. Also called a nadi.

Energy Plane—is the plane of existence just above the physical world that gives life and sustenance to it. This plane is full of moving energy, which has varying degrees of consciousness.

Vortices and Spirals

Energy vortex—is a vortex that forms in response to human intention and increases the draw/pull of a particular prana inwards to it. It either forms at a specific location or attaches to an object. Generally an energy vortex refers to a positive energy vortex and is a co-creation with Mother Earth; if so it may also be referred to as a natural vortex.

Energy vortex, negative—is a vortex disrupting the flow of prana and forms in response to selfish and violent behavior. It drains you of prana when you come in contact with it. It has a detrimental effect upon your well-being and spiritual development. When you are close to one, or within it, you may feel a variety of symptoms such as a headache or a draining feeling.

Energy vortex, positive—is a co-creation with Mother Earth that forms in response to positive human intentions such as loving, giving, praying, meditating and the like. It draws in a particular type of prana that is a function of the human activity or intention that created it. This vortex looks to feed you positive prana when you are within it, particularly when performing the activity which created the vortex. It is also called a natural vortex. You may feel a very positive, uplifting feeling when you are in it.

Fields of Consciousness—are part of Mother Earth's soul in greater central New York that nourishes us with consciousness. Ley lines absorb the consciousness emanating from the Fields, and then travel to distant parts of the world, transporting the consciousness emanating from Mother Earth's soul.

Gaia Circle—see Mother Earth Circle.

Geographic samskara—a thought impression that attaches to the land which looks to grow by having you think, or behave in a manner reinforcing its original intent. Also called land impressions, land imprints or land memories.

Geographic samskara, negative—is geographic samskara whose net consciousness reading is more negative than positive.

Geographic samskara, positive—is a geographic samskara whose net consciousness reading is more positive than negative.

Geopathic stress—traditionally refers to detrimental Earth energies, but should include negative energies vortices and locations with negative land imprints which cause major breaks in Mother Earth's field.

Holes, black holes, Wi-Fi holes—are locations where a negative energy vortex is, or is forming, creating a major break in the flow of prana and causing a hole or break in Mother Earth's grid/field. Locations where electronic devices have created breaks in Mother Earth's field, particularly areas where Wi-Fi technology has been employed.

Intention circle—is an area where a geographic samskara is created for a specific activity or purpose.

Keeper—is one who protects, maintains and watches over a particular sacred site and guides visiting pilgrims.

Land impressions, land imprints, land memories—other terms to describe a geographic samskara.

Law of Attraction—like attracts like. What think about or do attracts similar thoughts or actions.

Ley line—is a transporter of consciousness emanating from the heart of Mother Earth's soul in the greater area of central New York and beyond. In traversing Mother Earth, it interacts with the consciousness it comes in contact with in different parts of the world. Ley lines have been traditionally associated with sacred sites. Also called lines of consciousness.

Lines of consciousness—see ley lines.

Mother Earth Circle—your connection to Mother Earth, a barometer of the amount of Her emanations you absorb. The stronger your connection to Her, the more of her emanations you will absorb.

Mother Earth's Field/Grid—refers primarily to the Plane of Energy.

Mother Earth's soul—the location where Mother Earth's most powerful emanations of consciousness are located. The heart or center is located in central New York between Rochester and Utica, along the route of the old Erie Canal, extending into southern Ontario, Canada to the north, Vt./Mass./Conn. to the east, northern New Jersey/Pennsylvania to the south and northeast Ohio to the west.

Mother's milk of consciousness—when we meditate in a natural vortex we merge with consciousness of those who helped create it, and in the process we are often nourished by elements we were lacking.

Nadi—is an energy line that transports prana.

Natural vortex—is a co-creation with Mother Earth that forms naturally at a particular location, or on an object in response to positive human intentions such as loving, giving, praying, meditating, healing and the like. It draws in a particular type of prana that is a function of the human activity or intention that created it. It looks to feed you that particular type of prana when you are within the vortex. Also called a positive energy vortex.

Planes of existence—are alternative realities or dimensions that exist in the unseen world around us.

Prakriti—is the unmanifest, or primal matter through which the universe is created. It is energy.

Prana—is the life force that exists in the Energy Plane and gives life to everything in the Physical Plane. It is energy and is called chi by Daoists.

Pranamaya kosha—is the energy body.

Pranayama—exercises to gain control over the movement of prana and facilitate its movement and remove blockages in its flow; the fourth rung of Patanjali's eight limbs of yoga.

Prayer stone—see amulet or talisman. A stone charged through prayer, meditation or ceremony.

Purusha—is pure consciousness.

Replication—is the principle that the form and function operating in one plane of existence is replicated in another plane.

Samadhi—is the complete union with an object, of focus, during meditation so all other thoughts are blocked out and you loose awareness of the physical world. In other words the samskara of meditation becomes so dominant it blocks out all others. Samadhi is the goal of Patanjali's yoga and it brings union with God and illumination. In Samadhi our consciousness transcends the physical world and rises to the Collective Plane of consciousness.

Samskara—is a thought impression that attaches and looks to grow by having us repeat the particular thought or action that created it; in doing so the samskara looks to influence us.

Samskara, negative—is a thought impression whose underlying consciousness is closer to the demonic than the divine.

Samskara, positive—is a thought impression whose underlying consciousness is closer to the divine than the demonic.

Shakti—is the feminine divine power or energy that creates the world.

Shiva—is male, the lord of the yogis, the Supreme Being; the highest consciousness, pure consciousness.

Sick house—is a house with geopathic stress, breaks in the flow of prana, or negative energy vortices that make you sick. They are also referred to as cancer houses because of the high incidence of cancer that has been found in them.

Spirit Keepers—are those who once maintained and acted as the Keepers of the Fields of Consciousness in greater central New York. They preceded the Hopewell Adena, but by how much is not known.

Subtle body—are our unseen bodies that correspond with and exist in the various planes of existence.

Talisman—is an object which has been charged through focused concentration often for a specific purpose. The talisman picks up and retains the creator's intention, which supplies its charge and power; basically a samskara attaches to the object. The term talisman has been traditionally associated with objects created for good luck.

Transcending time—the process of connecting with the consciousness and being of those who helped create a natural vortex with a high consciousness component when you are praying or meditating within it. In essence you are connecting with the very beings of those who created the natural vortex in the past, and in a way transcending time.

Unity Principle—describes how a circle, a vortex, looks to merge and unite everything within it. We are constantly within a variety of circles--all of which are trying to unite and merge us with their other elements; in the process they shape us and unite us with others.

Vortex ring—is the final step before the formation of an energy vortex. It is a circling pattern of prana within a geographic samskara. A vortex forms when prana radiates in from the vortex ring.

Vortex synergy—is the increase of energy flowing toward an energy vortex when we are within it, performing the activity that created it. In other words, the draw of prana from our intention combines with the draw of the vortex, creating a synergy which significantly increases the total draw of prana of either alone.

Vritti—is a thought, a vortex, a whirlwind.

Welcome circle—is an intention circle created to welcome visiting pilgrims to a sacred site.

Working with stone—is to place and/or charge stones so that Mother Earth will be healed and or enhanced.

Bibliography

Sri Aurobindo. *Letters on Yoga*, Volume 22 SECTION FIVE.

Meher Baba. *Discourses*, Shaeriar Press: Myrtle Beach, South Carolina, 1995.

Dr. Robert Becker. *Cross Currents: the Promise of Electromedicine, the Perils of Electropollution.* Tarcher: Los Angeles, California, 1990.

Phoebe and Lawrence Bendit. *The Etheric Body of Man: The Bridge of Consciousness.* Quest Books, 1990.

Bhagavad-Gita; Chapter 16, "The Divine And Demoniac Natures."

Callum Coats. *Living Energies: An Exposition of Concepts Related to the Theories of Viktor Schauberger.* Gill & MacMillan Limited, 2001.

David Cowan and Chris Arnold. *Ley Lines and Earth Energies. Adventures.* Unlimited Press: Kempton, Illinois, 2003.

A P Dubrov, *The Geomagnetic Field and Life, Geomagneticbiology;* Plenum Press, New York, 1978.

Mircea Eliade. *Patterns in Comparative Religion.* Sheed & Ward, New York, 1958.

Ralph Nelson Elliot. *Nature's Law, The Secret of the Universe.* SN Publishing, 2010.

Vortices and Spirals

Dr. Richard Gerber. *Vibrational Medicine*. Bear & Co, 2001.

Joscelyn Godwin. *The Golden Thread: The Ageless Wisdom of the Western Mystery Traditions*. Quest Books, Wheaton, Illinois, 2007.

Francis Hitching. *Earth Magic*. Morrow, 1977.

Carl G. Jung. *The Collected Works, Vol. V*. Bollingen Foundation, Princeton University Press: 1967, Volume 12, #325.

Carl G Jung. "Man and Earth;" *Jung, C.G.: Collected Works Volume 10, Civilization in Transition, Volume 10, Bollingen Series*. Princeton University Press, 1968, c 1958.

J. Krappraff. 'The Spiral in Nature, Myth and Mathematics', in *Spiral Symmetry*, edited by Istvan Hargittai and Clifford A. Pickover. World Scientific, New Jersey, 1992.

Dr. Karl S. Kruszelnicki. "Black hole science key to WiFi," http://www.abc.net.au/science/articles/2012/09/18/3590519.htm#.UcCY7diurAw.

Krishnamurti Foundation of America, http://www.kfa.org/.

T. C. Lethbridge. *Ghost and Divining Rod*. Routledge & Kegan Paul, London, 1963.

T. C. Lethbridge. *The Essential T. Lethbridge*, Edited by Tom Graves and Janet Hoult. Granada Publishing, London England, 1980.
Sig Lonegren, http://geomancy.org/e-zine/1996/winter/gathering-earth-energies/index.html.

Bibliography

Janet Macrae. *Therapeutic Touch, A Practical Guide.* Alfred A. Knopf, 1996.

Black Elk. *The Sacred Pipe, Black Elk's Account of the Seven Rites of the Oglala Sioux;* Recorded and Edited by Joseph Epes Brown. University of Oklahoma Press, Norman, Oklahoma, 1953.

Masaru Emoto. *The Hidden Message in Water.* Atria Books, New York, 2001.

Winifred Gallagher. *The Power of Place, How Our Surroundings Shape Out Thoughts, Emotions and Actions.* Harper Perennial, New York, 1993.

Barbara Bradley Hagerty. *Fingerprints of God, The Search for the Science of Spirituality.* Riverhead Books, New York, 2009.

Alanna Moore. *Divining Earth Spirit.* Python Press, 2nd Edition, 2004. http://www.pythonpress.com/.

Clinton Ober, Dr. Stephen Sinatra and Martin Zucker. *Earthing, The Most Important Health Discovery Ever?* Basic Health Publications, Laguna Beach, California, 2010.

Patanjali, *Four chapters on Freedom, Commentary on the Yoga Sutras of Patanjali,* by Swami Satyananda Saraswati. Yoga Publications Trust: Munger, Bihar, India, 2002.

Maggie and Nigel Percy, http://www.professional-house-clearing.com/von-pohl.html

Michael A. Persinger and Gyslaine F. Lafrenière. *Space-time Transients and Unusual Events*. Burnham Inc. Pub, 1977.

Robert R. Prechter, Jr. *The Wave Principle of Human Social Behavior and the New Science of Socionomics*. New Classics Library, Gainesville, Ga, 2002.

Jill Purce. *The Mystic Spiral, Journey of the Soul*. Avon, New York, 1974.

David D. Robinson. "Who Built the 'Old Fort' on Bare Hill and other Pre-Seneca Structures in Yates County, N. Y." Crooked Lake Review, Spring 1997, http://www.crookedlakereview.com/articles/101_135/103spring1997/103robinson.html.

Swami Niranjanananda Saraswati. *Prana Pranayama, Prana Vidya*. Bihar School of Yoga: Munger, Bihar, India, 1998.

Viktor Schauberger. *Living Water, Viktor Schauberger and the Secrets of Natural Energy*, by Olof Alexandersson. Translated by Kit and Charles Zweigbergk. Gateway Publishing, Dublin, Ireland, 1990.

Michael S. Schneider. *A Beginner's Guide to Constructing the Universe, The Mathematical Archetypes of Nature, Art, and Science*. HarperCollins, New York, 1995.

Theodor Schwenk. *Sensitive Chaos, The Creation of Flowing Forms in Water and Air*. Rudolf Steiner Press, London, 1965.

Madis Senner. "Gaia's Soul, Fields of Consciousness." http://www.jubileeinitiative.org/gaiassoul.html.

Bibliography

Madis Senner. "Spirit Keepers." http://www.jubileeinitiative.org /spiritkeepers.html.

Madis Senner. "Foundation of Light, Spiritual Enlightment." http://www.jubileeinitiative.org/sacredfol.html.

Madis Sennerr. "Do Labyrinths Have a Design Flaw?" http://www.jubileeinitiative.org/labyrinths.html.

Adi Shankara. *Vivekachudamani of Shri Shankaracharya*, Translation by Swami Madhavananda. Advaita Ashrama. Calcutta, India Sixth Edition 1957.

Shankara Adi, *Crest Jewel of Discrimination (Viveka-Chudamani)*. Translated by Swami Prabhavananda and Christopher Isherwood. Vedanta Press, Hollywood, California.

Satyasangananda Saraswati. *Sri Vijnana Bhairava Tantra: The Ascent,*. Yoga Publications Trust/Bihar School of Yoga, December 2003.

Starhawk. *Spiral Dance, A Rebirth of the Ancient Religion of the Goddess*. Harper San Francisco, San Francisco, California, 1999.

Claire Sylvia with William Novak. *A Change of Heart, A Memoir*. Little, Brown and Company, New York, 1997.

Three Initiates (believed to be William Walker Atkinson and possibly others.) *The Kybalion, A Study of the Hermetic Philosophy of Ancient Egypt and Greece*, Rough Draft Publishing, 2012.

William Tiller, Walter Dibble, Michael Walter. *Conscious Acts of Creation*, Pavior Publishing, 2001.

Guy Underwood. *Pattern of the Past.* Abelard & Shuman LTD. ,New York, 1973.

Yogananda, Paramahansa, Autobiography of a Yogi, Nevada City, CA : Crystal Clarity Publishers, 1946 (2005 printing).

Index

CPSIA information can be obtained
at www.ICGtesting.com
Printed in the USA
LVOW13s1323190717
541887LV00021B/541/P